# Holy Moly Hiccoughs
## and
# Enigmatic Knotty Eructations
### from
# The Boffola Belly of Bu'Tai

The Drôleries and Dictums
of Crazy Modern Dzog-zen

Ken N.O. Sho

Printed and bound in Canada by Transcontinental, February 2007

©*Holy-Moly Hiccoughs and Enigmatic Knotty Eructations From the Boffola Belly of Bu'Tai*

ISBN: 0-9734439-2-8   ISBN 13: 978-0-9734439-2-9

©2007 Orange Palm Publications
Registration of copyright: First trimester 2007
National Library of Quebec
National Library of Canada

Mailing address: Orange Palm Publications©
235 Rene Levesque Boulevard, Suite 310,
Montreal, Quebec, H2X 1N8
Telephone: (514) 255-8700 ~ Facsimile: (514) 255-0478
E-mail: info@palmpublications.com
Website: http://www.palmpublications.com

Japanese prints collection, Prints and Photographs Online Catalogue, Library of Congress.

Graphic design and illustrations: Ken N.O. Sho, Eric Mathieu and Lucie Robitaille
Typesetting: Louise Roy

All rights reserved. No part of this book may be reproduced in any form without permission in writing from the author except to quote, or photocopy specific passages for the purposes of group study.

## Publications by Orange Palm Publications:

*Knots of Eternity — Paradoxes from Dadi to Daughter*. Volume 1. Dadi Darshan Dharma. 2007.

*The Smiling Forehead — Paradoxes from Dadi to Daughter*. Volume 2. Dadi Darshan Dharma. 2007.

*The Great Golden Garland of Gampopa's Sublime Considerations on the Supreme Path — Contemplative Contemporary Commentaries of Gampopa's Root Text*. Volume 1. B. Simhananda. 2005.

*Paradisal Plums: Peaceful Ponderings from a (Rebel) Pandit's Puce Palm — Aphorisms, Adages, and Analects of Sri Adi Dadi*, Volumes 1, 2. Etbonan Karta. 2001.

## Forthcoming books:

*Flyers from the Boys in the Buddhafield*. B. Simhananda.

*Paradisal Plums: Peaceful Ponderings from a (Rebel) Pandit's Puce Palm, — Aphorisms, Adages, and Analects of Sri Adi Dadi*, Volumes 3, 4. Etbonan Karta.

## Publications by Magnificent Magus Publications:

*The Divine Concordance of Light III: The Science of Full Moon Invocations from* Humanity's *Heart to* Hierarchy's *Will.* Etbonan Karta. 2007.

*Buddhas, Bodhisattvas, Khadromas and the Way of the Pilgrim — A Transformative Book of Photography and Pithy Sayings* (in three languages). Simhananda. 2007.

*The Divine Concordance of Light: A Handbook from Heaven to Progression Earth* (an integral excerpt from Collectanea One, *The Divine Concordance of Light*). Etbonan Karta. 2007.

*Seven Sacred Stations of the Self & Seven Flaming Fiats of Light Upon the Seven Cosmic-Physical Rays* (an integral excerpt from *The Divine Concordance of Light*). Etbonan Karta. 2001.

*The Divine Concordance of Light: A Handbook from Heaven to Progression Earth — "The Seven Rays of God: Seven Studies of the Soul's Earthly Pilgrimage of Service Upon the Seven Cosmic-Physical Rays".* Etbonan Karta. 2001.

### Forthcoming books:

*Scriptings of the Soul in Questions of Light.* Dadi Darshan Dharma.

*The Divine Concordance of Light II: The Science of Invocation and the Art of Affirmation from Station* Humanity *to* Hierarchy's *Heart.* Etbonan Karta.

## In the End

Let the present as future
meet the past as present.


## In the Beginning

Let the future as present
meet the present as past.

# Table of Contents

|  |  |  |
|---|---|---|
|  | Preface | ix |
|  |  | Days |
| I | First Hatchings | 365-340 |
| II | Second Hatchings | 339-314 |
| III | Stop! Do Not Applause | 313-287 |
| IV | Pristine Philosophical Apperceptions | 286-249 |
| V | Baba Brain-Teasers | 248-223 |
| VI | The Thunderclap Rising of the Golden Flower | 222-197 |
| VII | Free Energy Is Where It's At | 196-169 |
| VIII | Breaking Bread with the Buddha | 168-143 |
| IX | Cast Rice Upon the Waters | 142-115 |
| X | The Neigh of Truth | 114-85 |
| XI | Plastered Wallflower, Meditating | 84-59 |
| XII | Baba Brain-Teasers II | 58-33 |
| XIII | Quintessence of Creation | 32-(-1) |
|  | Eructative Epilogue Epistle | E.E.E. 1-6 |
|  | Glossary |  |

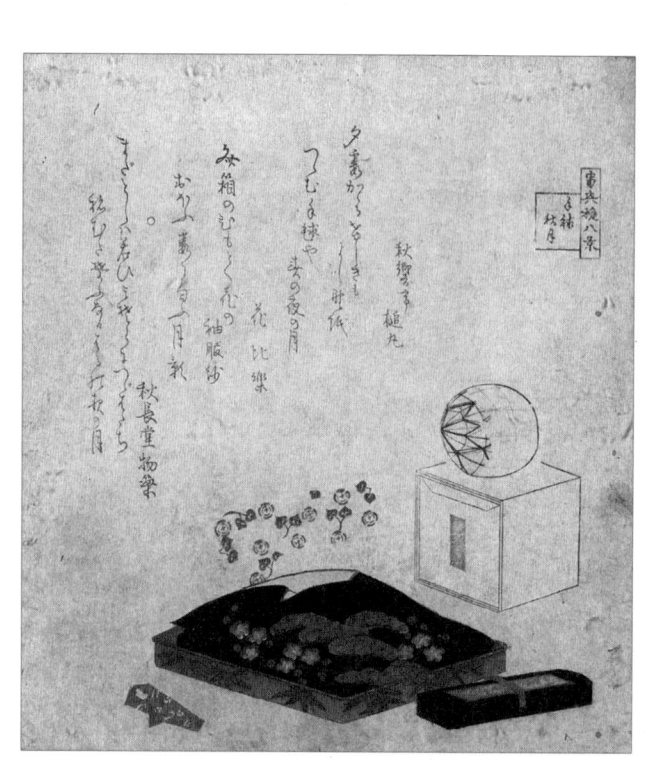

# Preface

Zen Buddhism, especially in the koan department, is sadly getting highly hoary and certainly crystallized. It exhibits an annoying arrogance and displays a much outmoded mode of koan-ic expression.

Some years ago, the author presented a timid selection of his *Holy Moly Hiccoughs and Knotty Eructations from the Boffola Belly of Bu'Tai* to a highly respected group of Montreal's Zen community, and ruefully, he was promptly dismissed as a misguided spiritual miscreant and literally laughed out of Zen city.

The author had evidently terribly sinned against the classic and sacred, (stuffy, rather), Zen koan tradition and was promptly, righteously, (and maybe rightly), ostracized.

Well, despite this obvious affront, or lack of respect paid to a long history of already perfected and not ever to be improved upon, nor ever to evolve beyond what is evidently perfection in koan lore, the author has nevertheless decided, (after ten years in solitary Buddhist extradition), to publish his little compendium of humble *Holy Moly Hiccoughs and Knotty Eructations from the Boffola Belly of Bu'Tai*, come whatever may be directed his way in the form of righteous criticism from the peanut galleries of various sacred sanghas around the world — from Montreal to Tin-Buck-Two, to Osaka, and so on, to holy Bodhgaya itself.

The little koan-like, paradoxical and somewhat knotty, (or naughty), passages contained within this meager volume will tend to break through the traditional koan tide and mighty Zen-ish dam which oriental and asiatic holy history has built-up, and western spiritual society has (wrongly) tried to emulate and follow with a somewhat assiduous, but naive discipline during the last fifty years.

The ancient asiatic Zen-koan perspective, which is traditionally used to provoke in the student, an intuitionally prompted 'kensho' experience or a directly apprehended 'satori' state... followed by a series of subsequent wholistic understandings and sustained contacts with the Void, (or Emptiness), that should unequivocally lead to the Higher Wisdom beyond... is not the modern occidental way of mind-deconstruction, mind-deepening, and eventual mind-transcendence, which should lead in its turn, to a natural resting in disciplined ease, within Ultimate Nature, or what is sometimes called, the 'Unified Field of Universal Reality'. Nor is it, the rest of the world's way of transcending conceptual perception through the common idiom and modern medium of the paradoxical symbolism of language.

Contemporary Zen, especially in the eastern koan tradition, is not the natural linguistic vehicle of the type of arcane expression which is needed in the wayward land of the West; and does not constitute the contemporary skillful means to attain freedom and finally Liberation, here and presently henceforth, in the Occident. The eastern koan tradition is not universal — it is rather, very asia-tically biased and easterly bent.

Buddhist Zen at core, is pure. Let it remain so.

But in the Occident, let it be so in an inherently, meaningful, westward land way.

This book appears to be the first, albeit perhaps, a yet awkward attempt at the creation of an authentically occidental approach to koan lore.

Nevertheless, it does offer a rather non-rational approach to life, and does present a paradoxical perspective to an altogether too factual, too apparent, reality.

The book's main aim is the deconstruction of the narrow, thought-impregnated corridors and engramatic corrugations of the mind... thereby enabling man to eventually demonstrate with a certain ease, his natural, universal Mind of Being.

It unerringly points the reader toward the experience of a subtle state of Non-Being, or toward an Existential Absence, where an open and spontaneous expression freely follows the way the Mind may work through the integrated personality as an individuated creation of the Manifest.

May all of you who are in various modes of seeking, or who have undertaken serious esoteric studies, or who are upon a path of spirituality, Buddhist or otherwise, give the 365+2 mainly paradoxical quips which are in this book, an unbiased break, whether you read them from the standpoint of an experienced, (somewhat cynical), spiritual perspective, or with an avid eyeful of healthful skepticism, or simply with an honest and non-judgemental mindset.

The comical Tathagata, or benevolent, earthy Buddha, 'Boffola Belly Bu'tai', bids you a good read and the release of a grand number of 'Holy Moly Hiccoughs and Enigmatic Knotty Eructations'.

May you chuckle, chortle, or cachinnate 'with a joyful noise unto the Void', or just smile tranquilly as you peruse, or devour, the jocund jollity and playful seriousness of *The Drôleries and Dictums of Crazy Modern Dzog-zen*.

And may the Suchness of the Buddha and His Blessings be yours in true Zen and essential Dzogchen, and in all authentic approaches to Mastership.

                Ken N.O. Sho
                Montreal, the 24 of February 2006

## Chapter One
### First Hatchings

The Boffola Belly of Bu'Tai

## Awake or Asleep

Awake or asleep,
In Heaven or hell,
In Wisdom or ignorance
Satori and samsara the same.

Far and wide, right and left.
High and low, hither and yon
In every nook and cranny of the universe
Look, seek, and find — emptiness the same.

From pole to pole, polestar to polestar
From the fair winds to the ten directions,
And in all climes and in all places.

And in exploring the whole of the tapestry of space
And in surveying the ubiquitousness of time,
tic-tocking over the whole shebang.

Awake or asleep, dead or alive,
Satori and samsara the same.

Everywhere and nowhere, noways and always,
the Nameless.

First Hatchings

Another Son

The Buddha bleeds to Life
every time He gives birth
to another Son.

Day 364

The Boffola Belly of Bu'Tai

## The Moon Pales

Suchness scintillates,
the moon pales,
the morning quails,

and a solitary whale,
hails a newborn baby's wail.

## Apple Pits

If pulverized apple pits
are bitter-good for the tummy,

forget not the palate's gratitude
for the apple's incredulous crunch.

The Boffola Belly of Bu'Tai

## Pretty Paula

Pretty Paula tripped prettily over a paltry, puny puddle.

Dry as it was, she somehow got all wet, and her pretty boots sullenly wept.

## G‍od-Dog

"God is a dog", barked Bodhidharma.
"Put a leash on him!"

And so it was that once upon a time, Christianity, which was full of fervency and dotted through and through with devotion, flipped God tail-over-end, (over and over again), until without a doubt, He incontestably became Top Dog.

And being full of Spiritual *sake*, and for Peter's sake, Epistle Paul put a Christian leash on Him.

And it was only later with a soul full of compassion and understanding for God-Lovers everywhere, that Mary M. found it in her kind heart to re-release HIM.

And so it was, that 'Dog-the-once-upon-God' vigorously wagged his tail in joy, and flipping over, tail-over-end once again… became just plain G_D… a singular Absence sitting in dogged zazen, in the heart cave of simple sadhakas.

The Boffola Belly of Bu'Tai

## No. 8 Tuttle

Hurry, hurry, Mr. No. 8 Tuttle
Come to the football huddle.

Time it is to tell the truth
to the Sky Turtle,
tuttling under your flying feet.

Day 359

First Hatchings

## All Sky, All Womb

On a clear cloudless night, all sky.

Claire is great with child, all womb.

The Boffola Belly of Bu'Tai

## Drive Through

Bare bones (in zazen),
please drive through, and toot.

*Mu...tely!*

Gadzooks!

Extinguish my flame,
light my fire, and gadzooks!

The Boffola Belly of Bu'Tai

## Beautiful Vase

No-form is but the beginning of Zen.

"Would you take a look at that beautiful vase, Claus!"

## Ketch That Hen

First, ketch that hen
in Ken's Kitchen, Gretchen!

Naw, the one beyond Ken's
already keen ken,
in the Kingdom of the Hen!

Only then Gretchen,
can you get to know 'KEN'.

*Cluck! Cluck!*

The Boffola Belly of Bu'Tai

Respirez

Zen/neZ… sous l'eau… respirez Mu... ffin.

Day 353

## KEN SHO Scores!

Tu fais du Zen à la Cana'yein, hé Emilien?

Tu pratiques ton Zazen à Montréal, hé Réal?

"Hé mon Dieu! Go, go, vas-y, vas-y!", crie Emilien.

"As-tu vu dat pass, hein Réal!"

« KEN SHO scores! »

The Boffola Belly of Bu'Tai

## Chirp

With painted bluebird in palm dare to void the vastness with a Chirp.

Day 351

## My Lostness, Ah!

The consuming darkness
has metastized into a
black brightness within,
and I have, (at last),
found my Lostness,
Ah!

The Boffola Belly of Bu'Tai

## Free Me

Firstly, free me from myself, oh my Father.

Secondly, free me from all (those) others.

Thirdly, free me from the way things seem to be.

Fourthly, free me from all slavery to spirituality.

Fifthly, free me from Thee, and let me Be.

## Bold Banyan Tree

How hotly has my heart
become a white fire
of bright bodhichitta.

How coolly has my passion
become a blue sea
of calm vairagya.

How lucidly has my mind's vision
of Amitabha Buddha the Beloved,
clearly become me,

Meditating Mu... mly

under the bold banyan tree of Coke-yu.

The Boffola Belly of Bu'Tai

*Erase*

Ink, paper,
and emptiness.
Erase.

Day 347

First Hatchings

## Tide In, Tide Out

Sunrise, sunset.

Tide in, Tide out.

Why?

That's Why?

*Gormless!*

Day 346

The Boffola Belly of Bu'Tai

## What the Heck!

"Zen and no sex definitely ain't for me," broods Tex.

"Sex minus Zen is paradoxically hexed," reflects Bess.

"Emptiness without form, how the Zen can that be?" queries Jess!

"Oh, what the heck!" gives up Ness, throwing up his hands.

*Gadso!*

Flawless self, faultless eye.
Nondual self, single eye.
No self, no i.

*Gadso!*

The Boffola Belly of Bu'Tai

## Life Is, It Isn't

| | |
|---|---|
| Life is sinfulness. | It Isn't. |
| Life is selfishness. | It Isn't. |
| Life is separativity. | It Isn't. |
| Life is suffering. | It Isn't. |
| Life is samsara. | It Isn't. |
| Life is slavery. | It Isn't. |
| Life is a karmic circle. | It Isn't. |
| Life is. | It Isn't. |

## Self Is, It Isn't

| | |
|---|---|
| Self is lust. | It Isn't. |
| Self is anger. | It Isn't. |
| Self is greed. | It Isn't. |
| Self is sloth. | It Isn't. |
| Self is envy. | It Isn't. |
| Self is stupidity. | It Isn't. |
| Self is pride. | It Isn't. |
| Self is. | It Isn't. |

The Boffola Belly of Bu'Tai

### Dappy-Dap, Zen

Dappy-Dap, Zen Dap

Hearted-hush hear Hum
Surding through muted
Moons of the Buddha's
Sonorous drone.

Haunting harp homophony
Hymnal holy hum
In hyaline-heaven home.

Skim-skirt-skittering
Like skua
In ecstatic skirling.

Ah, hyaline-heaven home

Ding dong dingle dome
Dap-dapping, dappy-dap
Zen, dap…

Like bedazzled
Silk-dapplings unto

Delirious ah-h embers,
Of euphonic Emptiness.

First Hatchings

## Piddle, Paddle, Phat Phat!

Ah, the big booming blue Void!
Hurry, hurry Dappy-dap Zen, Dap.

Piddle, paddle, phat, phat, but use only a ladle.

Empty do the great ocean of No-thingness.

Day 340

CHAPTER TWO
SECOND HATCHINGS

The Boffola Belly of Bu'Tai

## Nothing There!

We are all caught
within the tool box
of thought.

Open the tool box.

Nothing there!

*Yipes!*

## Shhh!

Shhh!

Behind the silence, PRESENCE.

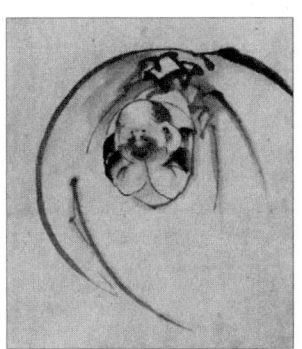

The Boffola Belly of Bu'Tai

## Everywhere Surprised!

Lend a serious ear to the CALM shouting.

"Hey!", everywhere Surprised.

Day 337

## In Ignorance

No Sensei, no pupil.

Only innocent meeting of
Innocents in Ignorance.

*Can such things be!*

The Boffola Belly of Bu'Tai

## Play Dead

The Ear hears way beyond listening.
The Eye sees way beyond sight.

Beyond the ambuscade of the senses,
Play dead, but sit bolt upright,

In Awareness.

## Hark, Heed and Hush!

The Sensei is nothing but an Absence;
do not talk to the silence… only Listen.

The Roshi is nothing but a Vacuity;
do not speak to the voidness… only Sit.

*Only Be: all hark, heed, and hush!*

The Boffola Belly of Bu'Tai

## Extinction

The Heart flames on,
only in your extinction.

## In A Rush

Real Understanding
geysers up
in a rush...
of no words.

The Boffola Belly of Bu'Tai

### In Saecula Saeculorum

Bourgeon, blossom and bloom... and a Bouquet of Bliss.

Blessfulness, beauty and balance... and the Budh of a Buddha.

*Wonders never cease!*

Bovarism and braggadocio are blown to bits, in saecula saeculorum.

## Pits of Prajna

### I

When the cherry tree blossoms and the plum tree blooms…

My heart is a perennial Spring of scented joy,
And my spirit an unfailing fountain of hope.

### II

Ah, would only that the glowing, growing seeds of my empty Nature mature fast into synthetic summer fruit.

### III

And, would only that the pits of prajna secreted within me, be spit out by my already fallen shadow… to take cubic autumnal root in the moist emptiness of the umbilical gap of my reeling refulgence.

The Boffola Belly of Bu'Tai

## Innocent Mind

An Innocent Mind is a constant opening out into utter Stillness, radical Listening, and free-arising, Non-Doing.

Second Hatchings

## A Blizzard of Absonance

Upon the peak of plenary accomplishment,

Contention, conflict, and confusion are all about a cramped base-camp, being caught in a blizzard of absonance.

The Boffola Belly of Bu'Tai

## Pressure-Cooker

Into the pressure-cooker of the mind cooks the person perpetually pretending to be you.

*Bunyip!*
*Tartuffe!*

Beats the Dutch!

The dreams of the day are daydreaming you dreaming away the day in dreamy delusion.

*Beats the Dutch, doesn't it!*

The Boffola Belly of Bu'Tai

## Heal Me

Hell Lord,
heal Me of me,
before 'I' escapes again.

Second Hatchings

## All That You Are Not

Experiment and explore
all that you are not,
then turn around quick,
beyond compare,

and be Naught.

Day 324

The Boffola Belly of Bu'Tai

## The Mountain

'Going up the Mountain, here I come', is a song of pure, spiritual, self-punishment.

*Well, bless my heart!*

Day 323

## L'Ego

The split-mind splits ONENESS to personal smithereens, and the personality compulsively picks up the pieces, one by one, and plays *L'ego* with them... in order to construct the conceptual puzzle of a psychological post-existence.

*lego!*

The Boffola Belly of Bu'Tai

## Existential Eructation

Naturally, if life offers a person
a plate of stark insecurity,
he will tend to push it away
for a sumptuous dish of security,
and thereby, protract an altogether
difficult-to-heal case

of incessant, 'Existential
Eructation'.

## Dumb, Duped and Dumped

In radical Forgetfulness,
where does the self go?

Dumb, duped and dumped,
and not understanding why,

The contracted 'I' can only sigh.

And the concocted 'me' only cry.

*Poor devil!*

The Boffola Belly of Bu'Tai

## Bird Has Flown

If you manage to identify the chirp, the Bird has flown.

## Bad Habit

To bade that the ball must bounce,
is a bad habit of the bobbing mind.

*Jerk!*

The Boffola Belly of Bu'Tai

## Presume Once

Expectation is creativity upon a crutch.

Presume once, and Life ceases at once o'clock.

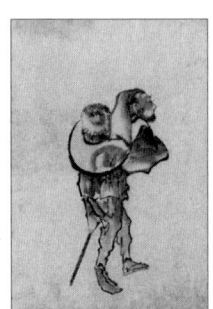

Day 317

Second Hatchings

## Scrambled Eggs

When 'I' anticipates,
the self vibrates,
the spirit dissipates,
the heart fibrillates,

and the admixtured ego,
decides to have
scrambled eggs for
nosh.

*Glump!*

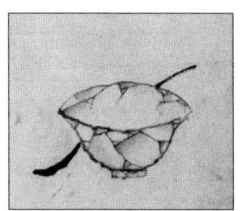

Day 316

The Boffola Belly of Bu'Tai

## Suchness

As the self abstains, Suchness bongs.

Day 315

## Last Illusion, First Truth

To know yourself is the last illusion;
To become your Self is the first Truth.

*Addendum I:*

To become a Presence generates genuine power.
To become an Absence vivifies veritable wisdom.

*Addendum II:*

To abstract into Emptiness opens unto a state of transcendental Isness.

To evanesce into Voidness translates into a legitimate vacuity of Consciousness.

*Addendum III:*

To lucidly fade away altogether from the Forehead of Existence,

Can be naught but genuine, guileless Aint'-ness... just Awaring.

CHAPTER THREE
STOP! DO NOT APPLAUSE

## OM Mani Padme Hum

Gratitude to the sky
for being 'OM' blue.

Gratitude to the forest
for being 'Mani' true.

Gratitude to the Trees
for (their) being 'Padme' pews.

Gratitude to the leaves
for (their) hospicing
'Hum' diamonds of dew.

Gratitude to Nature
for its 'OM Mani Padme Hum'
view of your Omni-Emptiness.

Stop! Do Not Applause

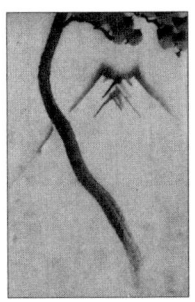

The
Stillness

Startles Itself
sitting
in zazen,
as the
Absence
of you.

Day 312

The Boffola Belly of Bu'Tai

Dare To

Stop!

And dare to address how do you do, to your not knowing how to do, without doing.

Day 311

## I

### *Pain, Hate and Jealousy*

Pain knows no color;
hate cognizes no body;
and jealousy has no bones.

And what is it that is so special with you,
my dear friend?

## II

### *Age, Anger and Envy*

Emily Envy is a green-eyed, (apparently) cultivated, middle-aged, (surgically-done), gorgeous gal, who has in her bright bag about 100 million, one-hundred-thousand begrudging bones to pick... all glimmering with glitzy emerald discontent.

Expressly what is it, that is precisely projected as being sweet, sensitive and sensible, yet remains ever so unnotable... about greedy, grungy, ageing and unforgettable, little 'ole you, Mrs. Emily E. Doe?

Ah, the art of putting life to death upon the rack of elephantine narcissism and pachydermatous non-compassion.

The Boffola Belly of Bu'Tai

## Same Difference

difference is Same difference,
and so?

## And So, 'Quack'

Who is there that can choose, or will his destiny?

"I really don't know", replied the little Zen duck.

"I have always practised just being a *sitting* duck".

And so...

"Quack"!

The Boffola Belly of Bu'Tai

## A Chance Acchoo!

Donald the dapper-dad duck 'delineator',
snugly and smugly enfolds cute
little baby Duckie, the 'defined',
within his mind...

just a bare microsecond before
really 'good looking', Daisy
radically collapses the
cozy image,

in a chance Acchoo!

Stop! Do Not Applause

## Azura

The body lives in the mind
living the body,

and how beautiful, Azura,
is the blue of the colorless sea.

Day 306

The Boffola Belly of Bu'Tai

## Fundamentally Free

Truth is fundamentally free,
whether one rides upon
a slice of white light,
or slides down
an icy chute of bare truth.

Stop! Do Not Applause

## Not So

Truth is Such, not such and such.
Truth is 'Ah so!', and not so.

*So!*

The Boffola Belly of Bu'Tai

## Between Two Bare Slices

Truth took me in my naked suit, while zen-mindedly eating a baloney sandwich.

And time tried in vain, to re-rind the transubstantiated baloney,

Back between two bare slices of concretized moments.

Stop! Do Not Applause

## The Opulent Open of Creation

Space charitably arrayed me
ubiquitously-everywhere-present
upon the great opulent Open of Creation.

But suddenly crestfallen,
I collapsed as a rag doll,
upon a shifting plate
of consciousness,

and dreamt that I was again
little 'ole me…

upon a flying-saucer of thought,
falling to earth.

Day 302

## The Self

A. The Pure SELF is the Quintessential Subject, the Original Face, the Divinely Unadulterated Nature, Which Faultlessly Light-spots Itself as AWARENESS, being Everywhere Conscious(ness).

B. The SELF as Consciousness Being-(Truly)-Everywhere, Is always Present for the first time, in flowing time, as both you and I, and the world, sempiternally intertwined and always arising.

C. Yet, the SELF, acting on an Inherently Divine Instinct, is also 'ora e sempre', counting backwards in constantly vanishing time through the same Consciousness Continuum in the capacity of a subjectively aspiring Self, acting within the arising awareness of a manifested, phenomenal incarnation.

4, 3, 2, 1,

*Zero, Emptiness!*

Stop! Do Not Applause

# Veritable Vermillion of Sound
### (A Continuation of 'The Self')

D. And whose individuated Heart yearns for the Causal Clarity of that ONE Eternal Moment of Absolute AWARENESS in Essential Emptiness... just prior to that Non-Moment, when the Pure Potentiality of the Existential Void vanishes into a Veritable Vermillion of Sound, and crashes kinetically into CREATION, birthing anew as the dark blue Vault of Heaven.

Day 300

The Boffola Belly of Bu'Tai

### Snow Geese

I saw snow geese
silently and magnificently flying
over the roof of my house.

I Honked!
and the sky fled in shame,
(never to be seen again).

Day 299

Stop! Do Not Applause

## I, Me, and the Self

The 'I' looks for survival;
the 'me' looks to the mirror;
the Self looks to kill.

*'Eh, Bill!'*

The Boffola Belly of Bu'Tai

## Yoga

Yoga is a communion with the known;
Yog is a union with the Unknown;

Yo is the greeting of whatever Is, in Felicity;
Y stands for the why's of the world:

"Why this, why that?"

"And why Am I, 'I'...

Essentially Empty?"

*(Duh, I don't know!)*

Stop! Do Not Applause

## To Be or Not To Be

Life is openly free to Felicitously Be,
or not to Be…

Below the bourn of Enlightenment,
or beyond the bloom of a Buddha.

The Boffola Belly of Bu'Tai

## Michelangelo

A Michelangelo creatively gives life,
to what Creation conveniently forgot
to manifest the first time around.

*Atta boy, Mikey!*

Stop! Do Not Applause

## Just So

A child is a child
because Life tricks him
to be just so for a while.

'Just so, little mother.'

Day 294

The Boffola Belly of Bu'Tai

*Stop!*

There you Are.

Move!
There you are not.

Move Again!
There you Are.

Stop Again!
There you are not.


'*Illusion, ah-ha, (I like it)!*'
*Illusion, ah-ha, (confusion)!*

Stop! Do Not Applause

## Lance et Compte!

You did not come here to score.
You came here to skate, and just Be.

"Merde, y' lance et compte!"

'There goes the puck in the net, again!'

*Holy ice bits!*

*(The Devil was goaltending!)*

Day 292

The Boffola Belly of Bu'Tai

## Holy Highness

Listen rightly to the Light behind your sight,
and you may just hear your Holy Highness sigh.

*Hoist high the Light!*

Stop! Do Not Applause

## Plan and Strategize

Program, plot and plan, and Life will bring you abruptly to an apology.

Devise, machinize, and strategize, and Life will oblige you to apologize.

*Sly fox outfoxed by rabid rabbit!*

Day 290

### To Meditate

To meditate is to hesitate before the Void.

### To Contemplate

To contemplate is to walk in circles around the altar of Emptiness.

### If you Must Meditate

Meditate uninterruptedly on nothing being meditated upon.

### If you Must Contemplate

Contemplate on the relaxed recognition of the Mind being inherently free, unconceived, uncorrupted, naturally spontaneous, and without nexus, nor circumference. Mind is all-pervasive throughout the length and breadth and depth of the Immensity (of Space), present without beginning and without end within the spacious Self. Yet, it is primordially empty as Light without ever having known darkness. And finally, It is radically rampant and intrinsically unconditional, (and uncolored), by the whole of Creation, and remains unensnared, by the slithering snake of samsara.

Relax and realize Mind as a delightful medley of the Manifest, arising effortlessly and flawlessly, from out of the Unborn.

Stop! Do Not Applause

## Projection of Life

Pain is a contractual projection of Life,
being all too suddenly, unwelcome.

*Ouch!*

Day 288

The Boffola Belly of Bu'Tai

## Do Not Applause

Poetry, painting, and sopranos
live and die in your Silence…
do not applause.

CHAPTER FOUR
## Pristine Philosophical Apperceptions

The Boffola Belly of Bu'Tai

## The Cure

The radioactive fallout
of original sin
scarred my Original Face.

The cure is in Remembering
it never happened…
I was in someone else's dream.

*Really!*

Pristine Philosophical Apperceptions

## Discovery of Self

The discovery of Self
can only be made
in the space that
suddenly got lost.

Day 285

The Boffola Belly of Bu'Tai

## Wendy and Joy

In your head the weightiness of Wendy.
In your heart the weightlessness of Joy.

*Weightwatchers a-hoy!*

## All Corners of Nowhere

The body-mind is but a temporal stamp stuck to the invisible envelope of Consciousness.

Inside the envelope, we have a blank page of translucent, dream paper bearing the Pure Land letterhead of 'All Is Emptiness'.

And the full weight of stamp, envelope and letter as Inherent Fullness is sent upon wings of Self-Awareness...

To the purposeless destination of Natural Beingness, which, ultimately, is spread-out to all corners of Nowhere,

As an Omnipresent Oneness.

*Air-Mind Delivery!*

The Boffola Belly of Bu'Tai

## Chase the Wind

Ashes to ashes my past,
and gone to the wind
is the whole of it —
why should you, or I,
chase the wind which has already flown?

Pristine Philosophical Apperceptions

## Null and Void

Do not seek to cerebrationally conjecture, nor make a critical comment about, nor try to comprehend the muse in me.

Do not seek to commune, compromise, conciliate, or concatenate with me, whilst I am in a state of abstruse *absence.*

From a pecuniary perspective, a concordant corporative conclusion was concurred to in a secret emergency conclave, while I was without doubt, corporeally there, although apparently bored to an unequivocal clarity of Voidness.

I also concur, that from the perspective of my being obviously present, but inherently Empty in consciousness, the said concomitant concoction of a concordant conclusion to sell the company arrived at by the crowing crowd of the attending quintessential quartet of concretely competent accountants, is hereby, rendered null and void.

*Sisyphus, Syzygy and Strong Inc.!*

## Unequivocally Shared
### (A Continuation of 'Null and Void')

After all, the majority of stock company shares are owned by Creation, and I, as the present Executive Director, have decided that these should be unequivocally shared by all the truly Empty Consciousnesses that seek out a simple living on this Richly-Endowed Planet of shared existences.

*Post-Contemplative Afternote by a Non-Existent Ego in 'Vacuous Void':*

It was from the visionary, viewless meditative nexus of the 'intense inane', regarding the Absurd Absolute of It All... that nothing material seemed to have transpired, (physically), in the company, and the only whimper to have been (eerily) heard was the receding sigh of the lost chord of 'I', softly evanescing into a suspiration of 'cipher, naught and out'.

Pristine Philosophical Apperceptions

## Pristine Apperception

The pristine apperception of a petunia emancipates the spirit from the impaired vision of an imperfect conceptualization of the false self perceiving the pretended-to-be petunia.

Day 279

The Boffola Belly of Bu'Tai

## O-Cipher Voidness

Light washed over me, and my ghost was shed.

Emptiness zipped over my O-cipher Voidness,

And Awareness took note and saw it very clearly, as diddly-shit.

And Consciousness, then unpretentiously relaxed.

And Mind, in a formal diddly-squat... meditated on Sweet Nothings.

Pristine Philosophical Apperceptions

## Light Hit A Bird

Light hit a bird and color came to be.

Brightness blasted a body and beauty came to be.

No Bright, no blast, no bird, no blue, no body, no beauty — Nobody's Bliss.

Candescence clipped a clump of clay and color cannonaded from out of the quadraphonic corners of the cosmic compass, conga-going and careening onwards to conceal, orchestrate, and commove the con of Creation.

A blaze of Bright burst forth in Bliss from the Beyond and bent a beacon of rainbowed Blessings upon this bodiless blump of blobbed insubstantiality.

*'Well, bless my Boffola Belly suspenders!'*

The Boffola Belly of Bu'Tai

## Bodacious Bluebird
*(A Continuation of 'Light Hit A Bird')*

And it was from out of that blind, blimp-base of unborn glimmerings, that a goblet of gobbet-bubbles, ballooned and bulged to the very brink of breath; and no more able to abide death, the gaseous orb bulged forth a bantam-boom of the most brilliant BLUE… and the once nebbish nothing, broke through the embarrassment of Birth, and became a living, bloomin' bodacious Bluebird.

## Wahh, Wails the Babe

Absolute Awareness arches down the chute of Consciousness and two-handedly grabs the individual spirit, and tumbles it down into the body as 'self-awareness'.

'Wahh!', wails the (helpless), human babe, in mock protest.

The Boffola Belly of Bu'Tai

## Jim and James

Jim accepted the fact
of his cancer
to the bare bone of grace,
and died healed.

James did not accept, at core,
the fact of Fanny's infidelity,
and lived on many more years, dead.

Day 274

Pristine Philosophical Apperceptions

## Skip a Rope

Once you personally interfere
with the events of your life,
as they are causally happening —
you can nevermore hope
to skip a rope like a Natural Pope,
or an Innocent Dope.

*Hosts of fried potatoes, and Diet Coke!*

Day 273

The Boffola Belly of Bu'Tai

## No Mark Upon The Sky-Clad Body

The memory of patterns past, of how it all happened, not once, but twice, and thrice in the present life, or perhaps, somewhere back in history, in the multiple throws of reincarnation's dice, matters not one whit to LIFE's ongoing Heart of Compassion.

What does matter for the erstwhile disciple, or serious student of spirituality, is to discipline his attention and to develop the mind capacity to take note of all (personal or impersonal), happenings as they (actually) Happen.

A serious student ought to take careful note of all his recent past experiences, and also of any old rememberings, or ancient awarenesses, wanting to be acknowledged, (each one of them, especially subconsciously), as being subjectively 'accepted facts'.

*Recollect, recall and remember all!*

## No Mark Upon The Sky-Clad Body
*(A Continuation...)*

Essentially, all memories (of pain and joy) are somewhat like the illusory scratch of dreamt awareness drawn along the interminable liquid back of the personalized, (that is, time-related) consciousness; moreover, from the grand perspective of Illimitable Infinity, all happenings are but timeless, pointless pinpricks leaving no mark upon the sky-clad body of an Impersonal Consciousness.

It is only after much such special exercizing of the Awareness, that it becomes possible for Life to go on unfolding in the student, without him.

The Boffola Belly of Bu'Tai

# CATCH!

An Empty House
is at once filled
by Life being at home
to Happen.

"And when I am a ball",
calls out Life,
"I have myself a ball!"

"CATCH!"

## Perfect Pointlessness

The pure purpose
of poetry and painting
lies in its pointless pointing
to the penultimate Point
of Perfect Pointlessness within.

Ah, the expendable beauty
and metaphorical babble of it all!

The Boffola Belly of Bu'Tai

## Elongated Entente

Absolute surrender suddenly skyrockets space into a vast Infinitude and vastness of Void, within the elongated entente of a skipped heartbeat.

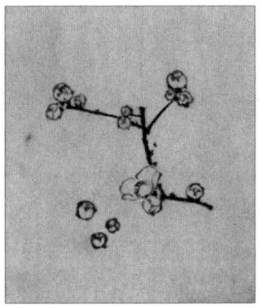

## A Paltry Play

Please do not point and poke fun at me playing out my life upon this specific stage of specified space, at this special time of serious purpose... for I fear that I could unforeseeably laugh, and thus break the captive spell of my rockin' relationships, or happy happenstances... (or whatever)... and prove the all of it to be but a paltry play.

"Tickets anyone, for a mere pittance?!"

The Boffola Belly of Bu'Tai

## Of Emptiness Held

As the playthings of the present and past go past us into emptiness, we sometimes pause, and become pleasureless, and sad.

But if only the emptiness could be held but for a few amplified extra moments, something more circumspect would cryptically pervade our being's wounded gap with an uncommon warmth and occasionally, a spontaneous fire conflagrates, and there erupts a pleasure perfect and a rapture pure… of a depth yet Unplumbed, a happiness yet Unexpressed, and a silence yet Unheard.

## Pretty Patricia

Creation as a phantom apparition can never be, nor ever stay; on the other hand, 'I Am' can never disappear, nor ever die.

Let us, for example, select the physical incarnation of a lovely girl, named Patricia.

Basically, pretty (corporeal) Patricia is but a lie; however, the absence behind Patricia is a truth; and the Presence behind the absence behind Patricia is the Truth… that is, the beginning-without-end of (her) innate, Subjective Reality.

This Original Nature, may be somewhat described, (as far as words can go), as:

Pure BEINGNESS… which is fundamentally Empty of all possible Qualification(s).

Supreme AWARENESS… which is inherently non-contaminated, even by such a subtle substance as Consciousness.

### Patricia's 'Essential Subjectivity'
#### (A Continuation of 'Pretty Patricia')

How can anyone really get to know Patricia, when deep down, 'objectively', she only 'appears' to exist in temporal time… and this, only for a short while, mattering?

However, from the point of view of her Basic Reality, (physical) Patricia does not exist, never did… no, not even Spiritually… other than as a psychic projection of Consciousness caught in the evolutionary net of Creation's involutionary arc of apparent karma.

Patricia's 'Essential Subjectivity' is her Only True Source of LOVE and Loving, but still, she, (as all men and women tend to do), is ever looking 'outwards' to be loved back to her SELF.

## Pristine Philosophical Apperceptions re. Patricia
*(A Continuation of 'Pretty Patricia')*

P.P.A. I: "Patricia":
"Your only Light is to live the Life nearest to you, with Love.

And what Breath is nearer to you than your own Basic Rest?"

P.P.A. II: "Near, near, near, no nearer can you be to your Truth, than your primordially Being, Patricia arising.

All else sought is but a sad going away from the All you Already Are."

P.P.A. III: "Your Allness is glued to you in Nearness, Patricia,

And you must become 'unglued' and totally 'let go', if surrender is ever to pick you up in arms swift and strong, and carry you back all the way to your Being Awareness, and Already Free."

The Boffola Belly of Bu'Tai

## Pristine Philosophical Apperceptions re. Patricia
### (A Continuation of 'Pretty Patricia')

P.P.A. IV: "The Source that you have always been looking for in love, and seeking for in knowledge, and pursuing persistently in power...
Is Nearer to you my Princess, than Patricia ever was… (or ever pretended to Be)."

P.P.A. V: "Waste energy no more Patricia, in forever becoming, more Patricia.

For before Patricia 'became' (unhappy), You were Already… just 'Being', (Joy)."

Pristine Philosophical Apperceptions

## The Great Gobbledygook

The picture in the mind, that of a cherry, perches precariously upon a perch of memory, or of some (projected), imaginary thought; then it is gone, gobbled up in consciousness by the Great Gobbledygook of the next passing moment, pressing forward within (the) mind a print of the following memory image to get agitated by, or to be identified with.

Constant inner dialogue of ideas and images come and go in an infinite, tireless procession of mindless pomp and parade.

*Gobble, gobble, gobble!*

Day 261

## The Whole Picture Show
### (A Continuation of 'the Great Gobbledygook')

Upon the absent subjective perch of a peach tree, perceive steadfastly and dispassionately, the hummingbirds of thought as they flitter forever to and fro... until the whole 'picture-show' cryptically disappears, film-negatives, and all, even the camera.

Then, as a ripple-less Consciousness, Being-What-It-Is Essentially Empty, and yet full of Mu, be at the Origin of your Creation 'on Ku'... and Smile — the secret SMILE (of a Buddha), caught within the cryptic, contemplative timelessness of an amaranthine Mona Lisa!

Pristine Philosophical Apperceptions

## Just So, Fullness

Vacate memory, and haul ass out of the past; take leave of objects, and become barren in Being — just so, Fullness.

*Burp!*

## A Couple of Nobodies

Subtract yourself from the somebody you think you are, and dare to be nothing with me.

And together, we shall be as One, just a couple of nobodies absently eating (a hot dog), at Joe's Pizza Parlor — for Absentee's only.

*Rules of Entrance:*

1. Eating only, allowed… nothing on the menu.

2. Talking only, endorsed… no words to be spoken.

3. Loving only, approved… (with) nobody to be loved.

4. Being only, sanctioned… (with) no memory to prompt.

5. Acceptance only, ratified… (with) no suffering authorized.

## A Micro-Infinity Later

As I drive, my car follows myself flying along the highway at the warp speed of my future, colliding with the present (me) sitting stolidly in my seat.

My energy body hits a (partly-hidden) stop sign, looks back at me, and raises a foreboding hand, palm extended in admonishment toward my forehead. I slow down and furtively smile, sheepishly acknowledging the dangerous, four-corner crossing ahead.

And then, a passably, meager distance along the speedy, slithering road some half a micro-infinity later, it is the acclivitous curve's turn to ominously extend up a crooked 'finger of warning' to myself.

I cringe and unequivocally 'accept' its crucial terms of circumstantial life-conditioning, or CRASH into that fast future-fated oak tree, where there, my energy body already sits, to soak in the Sun.

The Boffola Belly of Bu'Tai

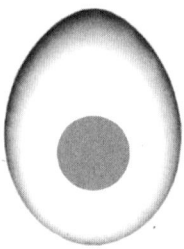

### Back To Square One

Offer up the nobody of self to the driver's seat and let go of the wheel of personal volition, as you veer hither and thither over the grinds, and bumps, and potholes of the Path which goes nowhere but back to Square One, before birth became such a Bright Idea.

*Boing!*

## Philosophizing

'Philosophizing' for a certain type of psyche, is frequently but an intellectually, impulsive addiction, a postulatory, prophylactic drug for a mindset too often perverted by subtle personal proclivities and a closed consciousness.

Assume, analyze, posit a premise, deduct, induct, dispute, argue, debate, rationalize, propose the pros and cons; dialogue, contemplate, cogitate, reason, plea, hypothesize, rule out, contend, conceive, infer, theorize, logicize, syllogize, or even generalize; and your head-in-the-sky, (seemingly) dispassionate philosopher will usually succeed in making things quite complicated — and not, of course, without a postulated headache to boot.

Two of the greatest handicaps to authentic spirituality lie in the (projected) obtrusion into consciousness of a so-called 'objectivity', coupled with the contracted intrusion of a supra-sensitivity regarding the phantom philosophy of selfhood, or of separate 'individuality'.

*Well, buff my 'Bufferin'!*

## Mummed Arcanuum

Real Spirituality Is, and will always Be, Essentially Subjective.

Give a listen to the following esoteric stumper:

"From the frontal cranial lobe, empty do, your mental load;
And thoughtless, thoughtfree, and unexpectant… merely Be.

And from the dizzying heights of the ancestral medulla oblongata,
At the far back of the now vacant, grey parking lot of the Head-Office,

Bank out instinctively, and freefall forward unthinking, and mindless,
Into the great bogus Void of the Illimitable Unknown of Inner space,

And thump down ever-so Lightly safe into the mummed Arcanuum of the HEART."

"Shhh." "Shunya". "Tabla Rasa". "Nada".

"Hush. Hum…

And Hold."

## The Great Waiting and Gestation Period

In the great waiting and gestation period which generally follows Shunyata, numerous themes of tranquil, post-meditative and contemplative practices are naturally, yet effortlessly, undertaken.

There are, therefore, in that which follows, a few such study themes in the form of questions, which should be skeptically analyzed, questionably explored, and profoundly expanded into some delectable Insight.

The personal Instructor, Teacher, Master, Guru, Lama, Roshi, or Murshid, can, of course, make-up a list (of themes and questions), which are far more fitting and favorable to his student's present spiritual status, or seeming stature upon the ladder of initiatory evolution; and which, of course, have to be more in accord with his personal degree of compassionate enlightenment.

Some equivocal themes which sadhakas and chelas everywhere can meditatively contemplate with deep analysis and consequential insight, could very well include any of the following cryptic queries:

?

## Study Themes 1-10

(A Continuation of 'The Great Waiting...')

1. On the Path, or No-Path, what is meant by the phrase 'unconditional Openness'?

2. What is the true significance of having, (or becoming), 'total Receptivity'?

3. Why is the 'absolute Acceptance' of life and its givings, or misgivings, an absolute must?

4. What is the relationship of all aforementioned concepts, or practices, with that which is termed, (or coined), 'Occult Obedience'?

5. What is the difference between Consciousness and self-consciousness?

6. How does Awareness differ from consciousness?

7. What is Mind and how does mind relate to consciousness?

8. How can the Mind be the root of all realities, samsaric and nirvanic?

9. Does the Mind have shape? How is its nature similar to space?

10. How is duality related to conceptuality?

## Study Themes 11-17
*(A Continuation of 'The Great Waiting...')*

11. Is there division in Emptiness? Why so, if so? Why not, if not?

12. By what means, or modality, does the true nature of mind relate to Emptiness?

13. How can the Suchness, Emptiness, or Realness of one (thing), bring on knowledge of all things, and of no-thing?

14. Why and how does the womb of the occulted unmanifest carry within itself the potential of (all) form?

15. As water has the nature of wetness and fire of heat, all things have in themselves the nature of emptiness.

    Contemplate this, and elucidate.

16. Is lucidity transparently related to clarity, and therefore, to the mind's realization of its own inherent emptiness, (within Emptiness)? Clarify.

17. Is resting with disciplined ease in Ultimate Nature, the same as samadhi meditation; or skillful concentration; or tranquil contemplation, with no thought?

*Hum!*

## Is This All Paradoxical?

Instead of always being robotically re-rooted and re-routed by recurrent thought, and of being reconditioned by the apperceptive philosophic appearance of mind flow... caught within the (projected) ramifications of a fluctuating consciousness undergoing (perpetual) objectification and modification, into a world of form and phenomenon... let the mind, in its natural response to the aforegoing, contemplative exercises, re-begin to think deeply, discerningly, originally, yet learn to rest all the while, consciously and completely, as Pure Emptiness.

Is this all paradoxical? Of course it is.

But only for those who are the die-hard material philosophizers, and ergo, for all those addicted thinkers who dine on the drugged food of the innate intelligence of the sacred intellect, and consequently, of the prehensibility of the mind to 'know' it all, or just about all, concretely and logically.

*Well, hoity-toity!*

Pristine Philosophical Apperceptions

## There You Are!

"Where I am not: "There You Are!"
"Now isn't this fun!"

*Let us play...*
'Pristine Philosophical Apperceptions', again!

Day 249

CHAPTER FIVE
## BABA BRAIN-TEASERS

The Boffola Belly of Bu'Tai

## Death After Doubt

D<small>ANGER</small>:
'Adopt Baba,
and the mind keels over
in death after doubt'.

Day 248

## Empty Mind, Purified Heart

Fetch Me not flowers, nor fruits...
for without the sacrificial incense
of the Fragrant Heart,
such offerings are mere objects
of sham spirituality,
and empty fawnings.

Float the ego across to Me
on the lovely lotus
of the empty mind,
and purified heart.

*Om Ah Hum!*

The Boffola Belly of Bu'Tai

## Earthly Experience

Proffer me something
which is yours alone to offer…
the perfume of PURITY purged
by the tears of earthly experience.

## My Only Gift

Without Surrender, no Grace.

This is indeed My greatest stipulation, and My only gift.

*Merry 'Xmas from Baba!*

The Boffola Belly of Bu'Tai

## Absolute Obedience

Come and stay,
or come and go,
I care not.

But I do care enough
for you to owe Me
absolute obedience.

*Om Shivoham!*

Baba Brain-Teasers

Babylonian Barding

Bhajan without Bhakti
and bhajan without the Beloved,
is mere banyan-bonging
and Babylonian barding.

Day 243

The Boffola Belly of Bu'Tai

## Orb of Equanimity

Baba has no love,
Baba has no hate.
Baba does not exist,
except as an effulgent orb
of Equanimity...
at the very Heart of Creation.

*Noble nexus of neutrality!*

Baba Brain-Teasers

## Labor of Love

I take absolutely nothing
from no one,
but do bring to Me
the labor of your love.

*'Working for the Man!'*

Day 241

The Boffola Belly of Bu'Tai

Busiest

I am busiest
when doing Nothing,
twenty-four hours a day.

*Holy hammocking!*

Baba Brain-Teasers

### Fair

Happy am I,
when another
brings to Me his burden,
for fair is the exchange
of something for Nothing.

*$2.00!*

Day 239

The Boffola Belly of Bu'Tai

## Till All Are Lifted

I have come
to light the Lamp of Love
by day in man,
in order that it burn long and deep
into the night
of a man's sins and sorrows.

This Baba shall not rest
till all are lifted,
into the Light of His Sight.

## I Have Come…

"I have come
to disturb and to discipline…
for you to discern and to deliberate."

"I have come
to disarm and to direct…
for you to discard and to decide."

"I have come
to reform and to restore…"

"For you to rehabilitate your self,
and be reshaped into Naught."

*Smart Sapiency!*

The Boffola Belly of Bu'Tai

## Quickening

All those close to Me
are mine to love into the Light,
and to chastise in a quickening,
towards Awakening.

Day 236

## I Shall Give Him

If a man calls upon Me with love,
I shall take away his name
and give him my Namelessness.

I shall give in his absence, my Presence.
I shall give for his devotion, my Nearness.

I shall bestow, with his surrender, my Freedom.

The Boffola Belly of Bu'Tai

## Again and Again

"Deny Me, and I shall go on affirming you.
Reject Me, and I shall go on accepting you.

Forsake Me, and I shall go on inviting you,
to come again, and again

Till you inevitably... *Evanesce.*"

## Baba Bears, Baba Upholds

"Baba bears everybody in Emptiness, within His FORM.

Baba upholds all appellations without designation, within His NAME."

The Boffola Belly of Bu'Tai

### Reactive Animal Animosity

"A scorpion straightens out and stings, a snake hisses and strikes, a dog barks and bites, a bull snorts and charges, a rhino grumbles and rushes, a crocodile crunches and chomps, a cat spits and claws... and a lion roaringly roars and springs in mortiferous attack."

Without Love, a man may imitate reactive animal animosity, and retaliate.

When a cat scratches and bites, should a man scratch and bite the cat back in righteous, beastly recoil and in retaliation of a wounded ego's vainglory?

## Better the Ear Not Hear, Better the Eye Not See

Preferable it is for the ear not to hear, than to take in and consume the world's crass cacophony.

Preferable it is for the eye not to see, than to behold and absorb the world's Babylonian beauty.

Preferable it is for the ear not to hear and the eye not to see, than to apprehend and incorporate into us the imitative world's spiritual impoverization of Ishwara.

## Pleasure of Purusha

Prarabdha karma will pass on
and possibly perish, but only
if we promptly and spiritedly,
proceed to impartially transpose
all performance that is personal,
toward the primary pleasure
of PURUSHA.

## Pristine Purity, Assured Eternity

The one sure date you can never renege on, is your destined date with Death.

In provision, therefore, endeavour to be Light-like, lamblike, childlike, undefiled, incorrupt, and clean.

Your *Pristine Purity* is your Assured Eternity.

Do not, therefore, inadvertently lose your Soul's highest virtue of inherent Divine Virginity.

The Boffola Belly of Bu'Tai

## Captivating Passion

"A powerful penchant toward Purusha renders all captivating passion powerless."

## If you Desire Me

If you desire me beyond anything else, you deserve Only Me.

If you heedlessly need, or rashly require me, (then) you entitle Me to do (whatever), unto you.

The Boffola Belly of Bu'Tai

### Indwelling Divinity

Man glorifies God as great and good and godly… but he gainsays to gaze upon Him only within the girdling of his own granary.

Man's dharmic destiny is the design, delight, and discovery of his own Indwelling Divinity, within the measureless vastness of the Void.

*Om Mahavishnu!*

## Imminent Nearness

Without the personal, inescapable perception of a noble mountain from a relative distance, you would never be able to apperceive its actual size, nor could you apprehend and appreciate its sublime summit.

BABA is such a Sacred Mountain, and it is only in the instance of His Darshan that He, as Shiva, chooses to shower down His Grace from the snowy summit of His Immanent Nearness to you.

The Boffola Belly of Bu'Tai

## Positively Poorna

The Prema of Sat Purusha is positively Poorna.

"So then, my Divya Atma Swaroopulaara's, do pursue Me with implacable perseverance, and openly praise the Supreme Purpose of Sat Purusha's Plan for the benefit of Man."

*Wonder of wonders!*

Day 224

## Sathyasya Sathyam

The wicked ones will not be wasted.
The wrongdoers will not be wrecked.
The apostates will not be apartheid.
The reprobates will not be revoked.

All malfeasance, miscreancy, and malevolence will be manacled and managed with *maitri*.

All baneful spirits and men of iniquity shall be made to apprehend their misdeeds, and to comprehend their mismotivation.

"This Cosmic Avatar shall compassionately tend to these modern miscreants and black sheep of the Kali Yuga; and they shall soon stand forth as being constrained, corrected, and re-educated... as well as (being) re-converted back to the original Dharma Path they have somehow escalloped from."

"So says Sri Sri Sathya Sai,
as "SATHYASYA SATHYAM"...
the Sacred Bearer of the Truth of TRUTHS."

CHAPTER SIX
## THE THUNDERCLAP RISING OF THE GOLDEN FLOWER

The Boffola Belly of Bu'Tai

## Take the Human Away

Take the human away from the Teacher,
and you destroy the Godman.

Take the human away from the Roshi,
and you destroy Nothing.

The Thunderclap Rising of the Golden Flower

## The Secret Is Out

The well-kept Secret of the Buddha is everywhere spread-out as the entire Manifest, Lightly-held within the beauty of a single flower.

And it is entirely spent as the whole Truth, honorably harbored within the hull of a single grain of rice.

*A single grain of white rice unseen, upon the yellow centre of a single daisy.*

Ah, Mahakashyapa, the Secret is out!

The Boffola Belly of Bu'Tai

## What Can the Matter Be?

One without me remains One.

One plus me perdures as me, with
a multiple view.

Oh dear, what can the matter be,
with little 'ole multifaceted, multicolored,
polymorphous, perdurable, and pointless me?

## Din of the Quiet

Beyond the clamor of concept, beyond the tumult of thought, beyond the shivaree of emotion, beyond the tantarara of action — the din of the Quiet.

Tend an attentive No-Ear, o sadhaka, to the thunderclap rising of the BUDDHA's Golden Flower.

## Obvious Solution

The Teacher will always remain an enigma beyond any experience.

The obvious solution, therefore, is to endeavor to catch Him, before he ever became anyone's Teacher.

## Dialing of Dharma

Truth is free but costs a lot... so much so, that in the case of Christ, it cost the people the Cross.

In the case of the Buddha, however, the Prajnaparamita's price to the people, was the correct dialing of Dharma.

The Boffola Belly of Bu'Tai

## Compassionate Composure

If in the throes of spiritual thirst, you drink the Christ's vinegar, only then, will you be able to comprehend the compassionate composure of the Buddha, as he coolly ate his bowl of poisoned rice.

## A No-Show

Interrupt the passing show, and time will surely get upset.

Interrupt time, and the whole show is a no-show.

The Boffola Belly of Bu'Tai

## In Time

In time, I will become a Buddha.

In time, this is IMPOSSIBLE!

## No-Body

We are all caught in a marathon dash toward death — WHO will win the race?

NO-BODY, no-body at all!

The Boffola Belly of Bu'Tai

## The Roaring Silence

In my mind, the dual shine and shadow of thought.

In my single eye, the scintillating shine of the light of Lights.

In my emptiness — the roaring silence of the mere Immensity.

## Imperfectly Perfect

The imperfect planet is the perfect place to practice perfection always Now, already forgotten.

Natural perfection is yours when you are imperfectly Here... in pure presence of Limitation.

The Boffola Belly of Bu'Tai

## Fall Out

Fall out of the moment — unto the Buddha's Lap.

Fall out of consciousness — into the Buddha's Mind.

Fall out of awareness — into the Buddha's Nature.

Fall out of life, (and its devouring hunger for experience) — into the Buddha's very Empty Belly.

## Princess TARA

Feel deeply enough the pain of earth, and the Path will (effortlessly) unfold.

Whenever Princess TARA wishes to be reborn, the eyes of Her Heart only need to fall upon the sight of one person's preponderant pain.

The Boffola Belly of Bu'Tai

## Contamination-Free

Satori is not the hard part.

Staying contamination-Free, is.

## The Butterfly

To be born again is a fact of life;
Being already Free is a truth of Life.

"Ah, the Butterfly always knew",
keels over the caterpillar, dead.

The Boffola Belly of Bu'Tai

## Heart-Full

The Sahajam of Hanuman is a Heart full of Ram.

The Christ Light of Jesus is a Heart full of Love.

The Effulgence of Lord Buddha is a Heart full of Emptiness.

## A Getaway Moment

Let go of lax thought and tactless talk, o sadhaka!

Uphold, rather, the shimmering silence of the Golden Flower upon the holy host of a getaway moment... and tap dance!

The Boffola Belly of Bu'Tai

## As I Read This

Auscultation, sight, smell, taste, and touch are all avidly feeling around on cue in the pure land of Mu... and as I read this, the 'I Am', alas, is self-compellingly compromised.

Day 204

## Nearness of Awareness

Between my mind and the Buddha's own, lies the mere distance of Awakening.

Buddhahood 'Just Is', as the mind gets lost out of time, eating a cool chocolate pudding with the nearness of Awareness, as yummy topping.

The Boffola Belly of Bu'Tai

Hum!

"I am a-this, or a-that, Buddhist."

Buddha says: "Hum".

## Roshi Says

Your No-mind is the Mindful Guru.

Roshi says:

"Drop the search, drop the mind, and drop the grain of rice!"

*Clunk!*

The Boffola Belly of Bu'Tai

Sit!

In the humus of the Heart...
there, the Bodhi tree!

SIT!

## Oh, Oh!

Everywhere the same, everyone the same, everything the same...

Nowhere to go, nothing to do, no one to know — oh, oh!

*'sdeath!*

The Boffola Belly of Bu'Tai

## Got a Match?

From the very beginning, I was that Buddha who got away due to amnesia.

Got a match, *Budh*?

## Moon of Mu

A bluebird flew bluefully across the sky of Mind.

The moon of Mu, mooned.

## Chapter Seven
### Free Energy is Where it's At

## The Apple Pop-Pie

*Observation:*

The appetizing presence of the apple pop-pie pops up from the primary perception of the pop tart via the prop of the physical senses, and the succulent awareness of it only passes out of mind conclusively with the popping down of the tart, as it pushes past the epiglottal post of the throat-passage down to the protruding abdominal paunch.

*Epigram:*

The pure physicality of the pop-pie appeared to be (spicy) apple, but its subtle essence was pure cinnamon Impermanence.

*Chorus:*

It all arose in Awareness and died in consciousness.

Free Energy Is Where It's At

## Salt and Pepper

God ends where man begins.

God begins where man ends.

*Pass me the salt and pepper, please!*

Day 195

The Boffola Belly of Bu'Tai

## Honeycomb Hive

Rest the tense mind,
yawn the great yawn,
and swallow the busy flight
of the bumble bee... quickly,
before the noon snack
happens at honeycomb hive.

## A Madcap Paw

Track the consciousness like a hungry tiger.

Catch it with a madcap paw, and crack its bones!

Then lick your chops with the shattering, concluding crunch of candid awareness.

The Boffola Belly of Bu'Tai

## Hellcat of Existence

Kinetically take-up the slack of Consciousness,
and like the hellcat of Existence you truly are:

'Roar your fury to the jugular of mind.'

## Zany Zafu

Meditation with mind is an I-spiritualized state of glamored passivity.

Zazen-with-self is a superiorly deluded form of serious I-dleness.

PURE ZEN is a wild wind of spirit splaying the Great Emptiness.

And I am a perfectly scared skeleton riveted to my zany zafu.

The Boffola Belly of Bu'Tai

## Instant Quench

I poured myself a glass of water and drank its image — instant Quench!

Day 190

## Surf and Die

When life is doing you and it is always doing you — surf and die, surf and die, surf and die... until you learn to Snurf.

The Boffola Belly of Bu'Tai

## Campbell's Could Never

In all things correct, there, the Buddha!

In all things incorrect, there, the Buddha!

Campbell's never did and never could can,
the Buddha's compassionate caress.

## Moon of Mu

Let not the old codger Mara creep up on your consciousness, and convince you that Creation is a mere crystalline concept of Mind.

Bikkhu, bong that Tibetan bowl real hard, and let Mahakala's vibes ring in crazy concentric circles within your little rounded skull... until the moon of Mu, finally *moos*.

The Boffola Belly of Bu'Tai

## Let Your Self Be Smoked

Get out of the smoke that 'gets in your eyes', and let your self be smoked by Life... living you, till you become but a burnt-out, nugatory butt.

Ah, but while it lasted, i was a good smoke!

Free Energy Is Where It's At

## Mu, Don't Do!

Truth can be recognized only by the True —
so Mu... tate, don't do!

## Terribly Rotten Teeth

Mind you, the mind gives up only when it sees that it is of no-mind.

Then Mind, mindfully brings you to the door of Insight — where the Truth finally bares its terribly rotten teeth.

## Awareness Smiles

Witness somebody, (or something), and indeed, you are.

Witness nobody, (or nothing), and the witness itself dies, and Awareness smiles.

## Only Awareness Can

Truth can only transmit Itself in the absence of everything else.

The chosen channel of transmission is the mindful and purified Consciousness.

But the Preceptor of Consciousness, although an ever-Real Presence, is alas, at a complete impossibility to Be There, as the Receptor of TRUTH.

Only Awareness can abide in SUCHNESS, as 'Sahaja'... that is, as Tranquil Clarity peering through the body-mind, squinting and sweating in the Sun.

## No Tragedy

There is evil, but there is no sin.
There is wrong, but there is no blame.
There is wound, but there is no fault.
There is hurt, but there is no harm.
There is adversity, but there is no accident.
There is destiny, but there is no tragedy.

## I Am Certain That I Cannot Be Sure

We invest heavily in sempiternal solutions which last till the next inevitable, stressful crisis.

We forever seek answers that will last an eternity... till the next irresistible, inevitable question.

Why not stuff all this silly temporization away, Now, into the pure beauty of life's Perfect Uncertainty.

Why not espouse a smidgen of the Ignorant Pundit's philosophy.

**It goes somewhat like this:**

"I do know that I know a whole lot, but I also know that I don't know much; and I intuitively know that I really don't know, (anything at all); and morever, I am certain that I cannot be sure about any of it."

Free Energy Is Where It's At

## Hairbreadth Getaway

When the sun sets upon a desire of your heart,
Thank the Buddha that the sun also rises —

Ah, a hairbreadth getaway in broad daylight!

The Boffola Belly of Bu'Tai

## Honor Him

After having bathed in the Teacher's reflection, stay not in his shadow, but dance dynamically in your own Light.

Add the Self of your non-self to the Teacher's already perfect addition of Himself to the Reality of Non-Being.

Add to his Subtraction and become greater in understanding, even as you add up to Less.

Thusly, honor Him.

## Zen of Blue

Concentration is the focused channeling of an applied mindfulness directed toward a spiritual goal in sadhana — a great vehicle, indeed, for the stabilization of certain esoteric particulars.

However, as with all vehicles, it is not such a good idea to lock ourselves up inside with the motor running, and set up some sort of psychological boot-camp, whilst laboriously crossing the especially wide channel of constant endeavor.

Concentrate for brief purposes, and get the Buddha out your cogital backyard, into the free air of Skyful Awareness.

**Crazy-Wise Counsel:**

"Get off your cloud of concentration and A.S.A.P. Zip into the Zen of Blue."

## Swoop of Silence

Tenderly take-in the world into your wholeness and close your eyes upon the ensuing White Calm.

Then exhale, and 'empty-listen' to the swoop of Silence, sweeping-in for the carcass of Time.

## The Crown

The innate Nobleness of your body is the crown of your Heart... wear it like a Buddha.

The original purity of your Spirit is the crown of your Soul... wear it like a Christ.

The cardinal core of your Quint-Essence is the crown of your Mind... wear it like an Absence.

## Zazen Goulash

Cast flesh, bone, brain, and marrow into the cauldron of 'sitting sadhana' with faith, patience, discipline, and unbroken mindfulness — and without doubt, the august Dharma Cook will slow-heat the coalescent, zazen-goulash into Kensho.

## Hair

'Split a hair' and Life is lost.

Heed the hair and Life bestirs.

Zen the hair and Life awares.

*Oh, my!*

The Boffola Belly of Bu'Tai

## Where It's At

Free energy is where it's at...
Be There!

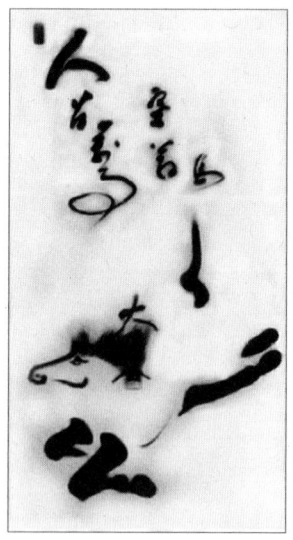

Day 172

## Knowledge and Experience

The kensho of experience is quick, Sudden Understanding.

The satori of experience is deep, Spontaneous Comprehension.

The nir-vana of experience is Direct contact with MIND, (or Radical), Illumination.

The gift, (or Blessing), of experience is the Inherent (Unitive) Light of all Buddhafields.


The kensho of knowledge is the knife of Truth.

The satori of knowledge is an Unerring Wisdom.

The nir-vana of knowledge is a Complete, (and Empty), Love.

The gift, (or Blessing), of knowledge is an Uncontrived Power and Unalterable Beauty.

## Love and Compassion

The kensho of compassion is Immediate Maitri.
The satori of compassion is Bodhichitta Enlightenment.
The nir-vana of compassion is Bodhisattva Service.

The gift, (or Blessing), of compassion is looking upon the Blissful Brow of the Kwannon Buddha.

The kensho of love is a Ready Empathy.
The satori of love is an All-Round, Gentle Inclusivity.
The nir-vana of love is a constant Sacrificial (Empty) Charity... raining Benevolence and Goodness upon the all of Creation... as well as upon (the) 'All That Is Not'.

The gift, (or Blessing), of love is the Empowerment of a universal Unitive Field of Love via the endowment of the inviolable Christos Crown, sitting delectably upon No One's Head.

## Zen and Everything

The kensho of everything is absolutely No-thing.
The satori of all things is a state of nascently Naught.
The nir-vana of the 'all that is' is Naturally Not, effortlessly.

The gift, (or Blessing), of the Whole is its humongous, Holy Hole of Infinitely Spontaneous Spaciousness... where everything just happens to be, 'Just Is'.

The kensho of sitting zen is a touching of Emptiness, or gazing at Essence.
The satori of Zen-zen is Mind-Not, (or 'Naturally Naught'), as Is.
The nir-vana of Radical Zen is sheer sitting in (blissful), Acute Awareness, doing mindless Dzog-zen.

The gift, (or Blessing), of Unadorned Zen is its spontaneous, open-ended Naturalness, and unified field of Ultimate Awareness.

## Chapter Eight
## Breaking Bread with the Buddha

The Boffola Belly of Bu'Tai

## Crackerjack Box

A diamond ring can come out of a crackerjack box, can it not?

**Is it really a diamond, Jack!?**

Breaking Bread with the Buddha

## The Sock

Bop open the box of physicality and
up pops the sock of spirituality.

Right foot, or left foot, Dan?

Day 167

The Boffola Belly of Bu'Tai

## Standstill Lotus

Blast out of the bilberry bush and jumpfrog breathlessly the standstill lotus in the pond.

**Buddha is in the water, not the sky.**

## Buddha Builds Highways

A dead-end, buddy?

*The Buddha builds highways through them!*

VROOM!

The Boffola Belly of Bu'Tai

## Rhythm of Reality

The whirling planets, the speeding comets, the shooting stars; the bubbling volcano, the running brook, the wailing wind; the swaying trees, the trembling leaves, the sounding reeds, the falling rain; the burping frogs, the chirping birds, the busy bee, the scritchy ant, the walking man... and his heartbeat — are all frolicking to the rhythm of Reality.

*The Buddha's head nods, and falls Awake.*

## Real Reality

Real reality is real magic every moment
a minute beams by... clearly Awared.

The Boffola Belly of Bu'Tai

## Halved Host

Break bread with Bobby Nobody and you break bread with the Buddha.

*Hallowed is the halved host!*

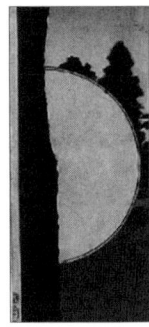

Day 162

## Golden Guffaws

The big belly of the Buddha beheld man
and blissed out in irrepressible Laughter.

*Bear to mind that the Golden Guffaws were
no phoney baloney!*

# The Boffola Belly of Bu'Tai

## And I Did What?

A body here, a body there, it's been a long arduous trip... male/female, who cares anymore?

And I did what... and why?

*The Buddha absentmindedly looks down at his fingernails and finishes off his mango.*

### The Nutty-Nudge

The karmic signpost that points, or summons, you to go this way or that way, stands deep to the hilt in pregnant silence.

Halt, look, listen... and sit.

You gotta wait for the nutty nudge that will hie you posthaste to the Buddha's chocolate-fudge factory.

The Boffola Belly of Bu'Tai

## What I Ams

I am so in love with I... that I never gets to be what I Ams.

## On the Red Phone

I am *here*.
It is *now* o'clock.

What should I do about
*then* and *there*?

Oh dear, the Buddha is on
the red phone,

Just about *Here-Now*!


*Can you feature that!*

The Boffola Belly of Bu'Tai

*Noexceptions*

Git it, git it, git it, you got what you got, gotcha!

Signed,
*Noaccidents*

N.B. '*Noexceptions*'.

Day 156

## A Baby Buddha

Just who planted that sinister seed, and when?

Why, I'm almost sure it was an execrable blackbird, or was it a maleficent raven, or a black-hearted crow?

Yes, once upon a shady lifetime, I was blackmailed, blacklisted, and blackballed by a blackguard (human) blackbird, or was it a raven, or a crow?

How puzzling now that my garden is such a mess. Damn that blackbird, or is it a raven, or a crow?

But wait, what do I see?

A baby Buddha has sprouted among the weeds!

The Boffola Belly of Bu'Tai

## Tithing

How much does a breath cost?
How much does a moment cost?
How much does anything cost?

Tithing is a universal law of life.

*By the way, what was the latest cost of love?*

## Zounds of Zen!

Burn brightly, bids the Buddha,
And remember to eat your turnips too.

### Pure Aroma of Coffee

My cozy and smug congeniality became rattled, restless and on instantaneous edge... as all of a sudden, the pure aroma of coffee, reeked of rancid roasted beans in bitter pain.

## A Plate of Plain Rice

Chef Buddha can cook up a yum-yummy barbecue burger for your mind, if you're ever shipwrecked on a lost island called your life.

But, of course, a plate of plain rice on the side is the apple of his eye.

The Boffola Belly of Bu'Tai

## To Cross the Buddha's Smile

No one has ever prevailed upon the sunset's holy horizon — except perhaps, he who has managed to cross the Buddha's smile vertically, upon the Way.

Day 150

## Mahakashyapa's Flower

Are you really related to the Buddha, or is He just a passing cloud within the mind?

If you are really related to Him, show me Mahakashyapa's flower, being gently held in the palm of your present-Now.

If you are not really related, no problem, my budding bikkhu...

They say, He died some time ago.

## Buddha Said: 'Children'

Buddha said: "Children, even if apparently on your own, don't go at it alone."

'Stop your lone dancing.
Stop smugly doing your thing.
Stop the incessant self-seeking, (even spiritual).
Stop the ceaseless desiring, (for this and for that).
Stop the self-indulgent free feasting and fast living.
Stop being covetous, miserly, and closed-fisted.
Stop the puerile habit of being hung-up,
on yourself.
Stop being haughty, puffed-up, vain and arrogant.
Stop the self-centered dissipation of precious time.
Stop upsetting and usurping other peoples' rights, possessions, and sacred space.'

'That is, stop all the selfish (sex) and silly stuff that disengaged and alienated adults do to feel validated.'

The Buddha calls everyone his *children*.

## The Princely Toad

Self-help symposiums are exactly that — 'Self... help!'

*And the real Buddha sits forgotten on some forlorn lotus leaf in the 'Golden Pond' of the Heart... alone with his buddy, the Princely Toad.*

## Two-Houses-Over

Think, think, think about self, and surely of mine.
Talk, talk, talk about self, and invariably of mine.

Feel, feel, feel for self, and positively of mine.
Do, do, do for self, and assuredly for mine.

With such an acute I-focus, the 'self-and-mine', quickly congeals into the compact picture of a 'still-growth' Buddha.

Spiritual times are swiftly moving-on, in an accelerated selfless sharing of the planet — whilst the 'I am', remains sadly focused upon the muddled mirror in the Buddha's bathroom!

"Listen attentively", chastises the Buddha:

"My nearest neighbor is the one suffering in Timararee.

My nearest friend is the lost one in Tin-Buck-Two.

My nearest beloved is the unloved one in only Two-Houses-Over."

## My Brother Kwannon
*(A Continuation of 'Two-Houses-Over')*

Continues the Buddha:

"Stay where you are!
Covet what you have!
You handle that well... too well!"

Suggests the Buddha:
"I will grant you the gracious gift of bartering for another burden in exchange for the old."
"How about it, little Bikkhu?"

Answers me:
"Hey man, much too comfy here!"

Retorts the Buddha:
"Very well then, I shall have to send you my growth broker. Her name is Vajra-Yogini, Calamity Jane."

Answers me: "Oh, s_ _t!"

Reciprocates the Buddha:
"May Blessings Be upon you child in both joy and suffering!"

"And oh, by the way, my Brother Kwannon, will surely pass by your place upon the Dharma Way, and give you an imponderable probe of Nothing notable, or if you are lucky, a subtle, bare buzz of balmy Bodhichitta."

The Boffola Belly of Bu'Tai

## Little Mu-Mu

The ultimate flight is Freedom.

Are there any bold bidders other than the Buddha?

How about you, little Mu-Mu!?

Day 144

## What To Do, What To Do?

The desire for the object of Buddhahood
is a doozer.
The desire for the subject of Buddhahood
is a diller.

A no-desire for the Buddha is no better.
And no desire, period, is an impossibility.

What to do, what to do, O Mahakala!?

"Nothing to do," grumbles Mahakala.

"Your urethra opens by its own self when it's time to pee".

Adds Maitreya with *maitri*:

"And always remember that Awareness rests inherently in Ultimate Nature, whether it's time to Be... or not to Be."

## Chapter Nine
## Cast Rice Upon the Waters

The Boffola Belly of Bu'Tai

## Mix Salt and Pepper

Hop in the car, drop the wheels and ride.

Run like hell but only ambulate.
Take your time, but make it quick.

Mix salt and pepper in a shaker that only peppers your steak.

Catch the ball, no hands allowed.
Throw up the ball, don't let it fall.

Jog on the sand, no footprints.
Walk on the sand, no feet.

Jump real high, but do not leave the ground.

Hurry, hurry, put the plug back on the pulled grenade.

Smash the egg to smithereens and retrieve the perfect yolk.

Make passionate love, but with no body allowed, (even in the mind.)

### The Buddha Does All Of The Above
*(A Continuation of 'Mix Salt and Pepper')*

Fall fast asleep, but keep wide awake;
Snore but with no sound.

Put the expressed juice back into the passion fruit.

Try to place the eaten carrot back intact into the ground.

Cheerfully reconnect the strawberry back upon its stem,

And rasp loud the color raspberry, but not without the bush, nor the blush.

**The Buddha does all of the above 'effortlessly'.**

[But so does Bugs Bunny.]

The Boffola Belly of Bu'Tai

*Ouch!*

Ouch says the earth pronged by a plastic fork.

Ouch says the Buddha pronged by the earth.

## Gracious Grace

O me, oh my, I fell from Grace, Grace!

Tell me my sweets, just what, or who, was this Grace that you fell from Gracious?

Gracious me, and how graceless of me, it was from Grace that I fell, Gracious, not Grace.

*Well, I declare!*

## Boris and the Buddha

Boris could not put the Buddha on the pillow.
The cat just wouldn't have it.

Boris could not hide the Buddha under his bed.
The dog just couldn't take it.

Boris therefore, screwed off his own head, (counter-clockwise),
And with a jubilant: "OM Namo Buddhaya", tossed it out the window.

The cat, with a cat's meow, and the dog, with a dog's a growl, both eagerly jumped out after it.

And all was presently peaceful and well in the blue bedroom, between Boris and the Buddha.

## Glorious Gloriole

The red, shiny, precious stone that Rock the Gemhound found got the full museum treatment.

The opaque, brownish and ordinary looking, power-rock that our Precious Lord found, got somehow, non-decorously tossed away.

Shame, shame, I saw the Buddha's glorious gloriole blush in detached dismay.

# The Boffola Belly of Bu'Tai

## Molten Morsel of Mercy

Support the Buddha's 'Foundation of Gentle Means'.

Why send a bulldozer to excavate the exquisite Jewel from the 'Cave of the Heart', when just a crumb of true Compassion will dig dynamite-deep?

**Conundrum of Compassion:**

If the Heart's gentle jewel ever becomes a chunk of cubic fructosan granite, clemently place the candy granite cube upon the carmine Buddha's tongue, and prostrating low... taste the One Taste of an uncommonly rare, molten morsel of Mercy.

Cast Rice Upon the Waters

## Patricya, Paul, and the Baby Buddha

If perchance, a pensive pupil feels plenty perturbed by the piping pandemonium of Patricya, Paul, and the Baby Buddha playing together, he or she must, upon the compassionate peak of a piercing, playful whoop, skillfully penetrate into the most perfect mind-state of contemplation.

Of one-pointed Suchness is the radically-open, random mind of ready Mindfulness.

Day 135

The Boffola Belly of Bu'Tai

## The Good News

"Every person comes full-equipped!"

"Now where did the Buddha sneak-off to, so that I can tell him the good news?"

Cast Rice Upon the Waters

## Lavender

The Buddha saw lavender and a lilac grew.

EMAHO!

The Boffola Belly of Bu'Tai

## Nothing Special

All that the Buddha can possibly do for you is to accompany you, while you sweep the floor, swipe the mirror, and scrub your mind.

Nothing special.

## Cast Rice

'Cast rice into the fire and you get back Rice Krispies', *snaps* the Buddha.

At that very moment, cousin Ananda crispely crackles-forth the spontaneously joyful "Ah so!" of some new sutra.

And the very mysterious Mahakashyapa, with a silly smile, just pleasure *pops* a (whole) rice paddy... in the humble crucible of his conjuring palm.

## And Did You Bring the Wine?

"Cast pepperoni into the wheat fields and you, no doubt, get back a Pizza", proselytizes the Pope.

"Quite so. The pizza is very Catholic in scope and very Christian in taste," remarks the Buddha.

"Do you wish another piece, my Friend?"

"Why yes, thank you, my Brother", replies the Christ. "You know, pizza has always had my paradisal, palatial Blessings."

The Lord Buddha nods, broadly grinning His very best Mona Lisa smile.

Master Jesus Christ continues:

"This popular manner of creatively casting succulent food upon a tantalizingly tasty, rounded-plate of Bread, and then to toss it over the holy heat of heaven's hell for pure-gatorial leavening, is an excellent idea for the new Celebration of my present Body, in a modern 'Host-Form.'"

"And did you bring the Wine this time, my Lord?", teased the Buddha.

## Cast Your Body Upon the Buddha

Cast your spirit upon Sound and it comes back a Silence.
Cast your soul upon Light and it comes back a Clarity,

Cast your mind upon Mind and it comes back an Emptiness.
Cast your body upon the Buddha and it comes back abloom with Body-chitta.

## Lucky No-Body

If your mind has a question, question it, till your Heart answers.

If your heart has an answer, answer it, till your Mind questions.

If you mindfully have the Buddha, dear heart, just naturally play stupid, you lucky no-body.

## Buddha-Buick Body-Mind

A Buddha-Buick, Body-Mind betokens an obligatory, lifetime-warrantee of selfless service, compassionate caring, and guaranteed sangha-sharing... as well as doing unceasing satsang all the way to the end of the dharma road.

Only then, can a sudden, slow illumination, happen at the first STOP sign, Quintessentially Seen.

*Scree-ee-ch!*

## The Full Moon of May

"Tweet, tweet, tweet", always sweet, always *maitri*, always merry, always full of glee... pipes the tiny-wee Bodhi-Bird.

Hear, hear, hear the spirited cheer of the already Free, on the limb of the nearest Bo-Tree, in the backyard of your own Illumined Mind.

Shakyamuni did, and never again, did He slump in sleep under the gentle rays of the full moon of May.

## Correctly Be, And Perfectly Love

Buddha proclaimed:
'Correctly Be, or not to be.'

Christ, in his turn, disclosed:
'Perfectly Love, or (you) love not.'

The Boffola Belly of Bu'Tai

## It Hurts So Good

May all of your talents use you.

May the all of Life consume you.

May the Lord Buddha abuse you.

Thank you.  Thank you.

'It hurts so good.'

## Cerumexed Ear

Every seven seconds, every seven minutes, every seven hours, every seven days, every seven weeks, every seven months, every seven years, every seven lifetimes, the Buddha blows His conch into your cerumexed ear.

The Boffola Belly of Bu'Tai

## Buddha McGee

"Whyfore a guru", queries the Radiant One, "when you have big-bellied Me and the one-and-only Buddha McGee?"

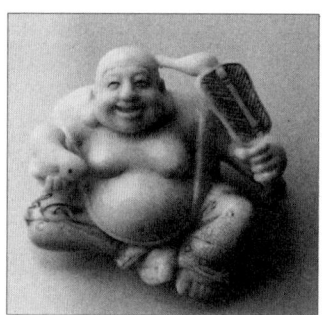

# The Mighty Buddha Exhales

The Mighty Buddha inhales space with the highest of glee, and lots of Muni Muni.

The Mighty Buddha exhales most Mindfully, and from out of one nostril pops-out a field of dandelions, and from out of the other, a gentle Boston terrier.

The Boffola Belly of Bu'Tai

## Ache of Existence

Within the great, big boffola-belly of Boddhisattva Bu'Tai, hibernates the lonely, painful, empty Ache of Existence.

*Shiver my timbers!*

## Spiritual Puberty

Upon the Tree of Life, the birth pangs of a brand new you bares forth a totally bored, Buddha-burgeon.

*Ah, the rut of spiritual puberty!*

The Boffola Belly of Bu'Tai

## The Bodhgaya Brinks

To actually behold the Golden Buddha is to rob the Bodhgaya Brinks.

Bob did it, and the poor boy is now wanted 'dead or Awake'.

## So Far Away

When Bill got to the Bodhi Tree, he beheld a broken-down, dumb Buddha, sitting in sloppy zazen.

He cynically commented to Betsy-Sue that the old man was absurdedly broken in body and spirit, and devoid of any real hope for true Liberation.

"Boo-hoo-hoo", balled Brenda, "If that's the case, I want to go back home to the Brandon I abandoned."

The small group that accompanied her, also felt disappointed, and with the exception of Joy and Bo, the group's members were discernably sad to have been so deceived.

They all had come from so far away, to meet the highly bragged about Bodhisattva Buddha!

# The Boffola Belly of Bu'Tai

*KYE HO!*

## Joyous Joy and Believin' Bo
### (A Continuation of 'So Far Away')

But late that same night, the broken-and-bent Buddha appeared in a dream to Joyous Joy.

Straightening-up, He so sweetly-smiled, and tenderly-tended His Open Palm in peaceful Blessings to her:

"Peace unto you, gentle Anandi."

And to her loyal and committed husband, "Believin' Bo", He bowed in noble Gassho, and also gave Grace.

At the same time, in the backyard birch-tree back home, a bluejay jayed in joy for Joy, and bobbed its head up-and-down for Believin' Bo.

The moon of May was Buddha-full.

## Nobody's Perfect

The Buddha's preferred response to a tough question is a nonchalant shrug, or an empty Voidness, — but hey, you know, nobody's perfect!

CHAPTER TEN
THE NEIGH OF TRUTH

The Boffola Belly of Bu'Tai

## Phat! Phat! Phat!

"Want to go to the movies", queries the Buddha?
"Sure", says Bonnie.

It was of me falling, and getting hurt, and crying, and getting up again, and falling again; and getting sick, and growing old, and dying, and coming back, etcetera, etcetera.

Holy Moly, it was only a movie, and the hot dogs and popcorn were really good!

Afterwards, the Buddha and I, arm in arm, did a duet of:

"Oh dear, what can the matter be...?

Phat! Phat! Phat!"

## Don't Want To Look

"It is obvious you are going
in the wrong direction, Jane."

"I don't want to look."

"Why?" queried the Buddha.

"In case you are right."

And so, bloomin' tired and in the dark,
Jane sat on a barbed cactus,

And the Buddha moaned in pain.

## I Don't Believe It!

You are a lamb in a pen; you are a zebra in a zoo.

You are a dog on a leash; you are a horse in harness.

You are a robot in human habit; you are a poor pea in a pod of perception.

"I don't believe it, Mr. Buddha, not for a minute!"

## The Woman in Red

'OM Mani Padme Hum'...

"You are now healed, my dear", intoned the Buddha.

"Hum, wow, that's very true!"

"A miracle!", cried out the woman in red.

"But now, what to do about the rest of my miserable life, Lord?"

The Boffola Belly of Bu'Tai

## Dharma Donut

How in the name of holy compassion can the Buddha generously give a dharma donut to a starving man... who then insists on permanently camping in the donut's existential hole?

The Neigh of Truth

## Last Terrible Knot

"Having no ties is the last terrible knot, Ananda."

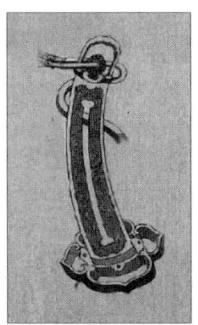

*Supasa!*

Day 109

The Boffola Belly of Bu'Tai

*Twang!*

The pleasure of pain is dumped by the dropping of the pang.

'Twang', went the Buddha's vica!

## On the Rim of Mu

"Sanyasin Jim is a real dream, and so-o-o very sweet," moons Sister Sheila.

"That so!" says Sesshin Slim.

"Brother Tim, could you be so kind as to read to us Dogen's teisho on relative Truth. Thank you."

And then some time later while doing zazen:

"Hum, hum, hum... what to do, what to do?", sighs Sister Sheila... pulling alternatively, and hesitatingly, on the petals of the mind's plastic daisy.

The Zazen Buddha, in His purposely taking position on the rim of Mu, there and then, falls unblinkingly into Time.

## Twenty-Six Years After

The Buddha did not seem to know all that much when I started to study Zen.

Funny, how some eight years later, he appeared to know a lot more.

And how, now, some twenty-six years after I first began to study Buddhism, he seems presently, at last ready... for my sudden Awakening.

The Neigh of Truth

## Upanishad

Do not bewilder a babe at the bosom, with bland Buddha tellings.

Ask the babe for the Truth, then do Upanishad.

*Goo-goo, gah-gah, g'loo!*

*Baby Buddha sutra, Book 1, verse 238-9.*

# The Boffola Belly of Bu'Tai

## Just In Time

Time heals not wound, nor sorrow.

Hurt may go into hiding for a while, but its ghost stays very much alive.

The predilection of the ghost to haunt the present, depreciates not with the advance of years.

And the phantom of deep-felt pain is never penitent.

"Nope, time certainly does not release hurt", construes the chastised ostrich, finally pulling its head out of the sand... just in time to see the Buddha chop it off!

## Open Gaze of Heaven

Heaven has no hands, yet how deeply it touches our being!

In similar fashion, as the Buddha draws near with no physical hands, He becomes as the open gaze of Heaven upon our hearts.

*Kye ho!*

The Boffola Belly of Bu'Tai

## The Blessed Beast

My first love was absolutely beautiful, but she ran off with Prince Siddhartha.

My second love was absolutely gorgeous, but she ran off with Siddha Gautama.

My last love was absolutely exquisite, but she ran off with Lord Buddha.

The Blessed Beast in me then died!

The Neigh of Truth

## Baby Buddha Fingers

When Baby Buddha enters my room everything smiles... even my bedspread.

Hey, give an ear to the 'ole codger on the canopy, who can't stop gurgling Mu because he got to be tickled by Baby Buddha fingers.

Day 101

The Boffola Belly of Bu'Tai

## Mean Zen on the Base

The Buddha postage stamp that stuck to my forehead, guaranteed my being expressly transported from Tallahassee to Bodhgaya.

But to my utter surprise, I found Elvis already there, Kundalini-shakin' in the lotus asana right under the Bodhi tree.

And there he was belting out 'Sweet Surrender', and being accompanied by Bo-Didley, who was strumming some mean Zen on the base, in svelte, blue suede sandals.

## 'BON' Appétit!

Ten thousand people per month go casually by a certain enlightened lamppost, on their way to the now famous Reuben's Restaurant, in New York, N.Y... for a quick lunch.

So strange to see how the Buddha's light burns bright in the broadest daylight, even as Willy Winky Walkman, coolly hip-hops and rock-and-rolls on by, on glitzy dharma rollerblades.

Ten thousand people per month go casually by a certain enlightened lamppost on their way to lunch in New York.

As there exists a particular meeting and eating tradition in Tibet, it could be said to all the friendly New Yorkers on the path to their noonday culinary repast:

"Tashi delek and a hearty 'BON' appétit!"

The Boffola Belly of Bu'Tai

## Big John and Venerable Obaku

After he met Brother Bodhidharma, Big John the Lumberjack laid down his axe, and after uprooting the one last big tree left in his own left eye, he set-up the Singular Lookout of 'The Fierce Attention'.

And it was only after years of fierce sitting at the 'Lookout', that Big John's silence roared so loud that it caught Venerable Obaku's attention a little further up on the summit.

Being suspiciously skeptical, the legendary Venerable descended from his Mountain Peak, and peered deeply-curious into the dank darkness of John's doorway, and Pow!

Big John had hit Obaku right smack in the forehead with a vanilla-almond Häagen Dazs.

# The Neigh of Truth

## Shunya, the Sunflower

Merry, merry, seems Mary Contrary.

**The mask is a fact of the face; the truth is a hidden of life.**

Shunya the Sunflower again forgot to put on her make-up, as she tilted-up her shy gaze, unabashed, to her Sun Lord, and surrendered the fact of her face.

## No Greater Faith

People put their trust in their own egotism; usually, they do not place their faith in the Truth.

People trust mostly their own selves, but not really the reality of the Non-self.

The Buddha trusts no one at all, nor really believes in anything.

Yet, no greater Faith has ever dared walk the planet earth.

## The Flavor of Her Ice Cream

The Buddha continued his conversation on "Being There" with Robbie Rahula, while chewing delightedly on a mango and peanut-butter sandwich:

"The whole of life is but a series of happy happenstances and a bunch of serendipity encounters, a kaleidoscope of karmic, criss-crossing, samsaric currents and of seemingly random, relational conditions... coming together on some particular street corner of the Path, (or No-Path), and then, o-o-ops!"

"O-o-ops what!?" said Jesus in a clear voice, as He came striding out of Bodhgaya's Baskin-Robbins, with a lovely young lady in tow.

She was blond, had on a white raincoat, carried a beige umbrella, and the flavor of her ice cream was Robbie Rahulas favorite.

*Holy Christmas!*

The Boffola Belly of Bu'Tai

## Some Time Later
### (A Continuation of 'The Flavor of Her Ice Cream')

Their eyes locked in a lightning conjunction of instant, (unremembered), Recognition.

Her knees kinda buckled, and her mind, (lumpishly), melted into mush.

His, (usually resistant), balls got metaphorically kicked, and his mind went kinda berserker-blank.

Some time later, methinks I was born.

## Never There

The only expert in egotism is one's self,
and he is all too happy to be always here.

The only adept of the Truth is nobody,
and he is never there.

*Eegads!*

The Boffola Belly of Bu'Tai

## Neigh of Truth!

Does the Buddha wear spurs on his sandals,
And would He use them on His young stallions?

Ah, the wild, jarring neigh of TRUTH!

## 'That's Life!'

Self-will is disaffected, dangerous, separative and poisonous.

But man treats self-will mostly as a healthful expression of individualism, and as an essential ingredient of actualized, or real independence.

Error is often blind and dumb, often misbehaving and hurtful, often misleading and estranging, but man treats it as an action most human and normal; often misread, often misconstrued, obviously mistaken, but basically O.K., and sometimes, in retrospect, even life-enhancing.

Harm is usually uncompassionate, non-caring, and oftentimes, borderline cruel.

Hurting someone is innately heart-hostile; but man treats it all too often as 'righteous', and 'not really ill-intentioned'; and too often, he shrugs it off as 'it just had to happen', or 'it had to be that way'.

And ladies and gentlemen, in retrospect, 'That's Life'!

*Well, I'll be!*

The Boffola Belly of Bu'Tai

## Fast Friends

Romantic love is short-lived and delusionary, but man treats it, as if it was really real, and lasting.

And so on, and on, and on, and on.

**The Buddha demurely decides to speak to the sleeping crowd:**

"How strange!"

"Man has made of Reality his enemy.
Man has made of Truth his foe.
Man has made of Compassion his opponent."

"And because of basic ignorance, man's destiny has become fast friends with Mara, and with his own nescient downfall."

*Sigh!*

# Ah Aprajna!
### (A Continuation of 'Fast Friends')

"And Mara, sly as he is, has somehow fructuously mated man to maya."

"And maya and man, after passing passionate ages of living in contentious concubinage, have finally married."

"And Mara and his deleterious forces, with their legionary demons of wrong thought, wrong emotion and wrong action, now consciously manipulate unconscious man at will, for their own base, ignominious and involutionary schemes."

"Ah, Aprajna!"

The Boffola Belly of Bu'Tai

### Fill-Up the Cups with Empty
*(A Continuation of 'Fast Friends')*

And the Buddha, hesitatingly, spoke on:

"But I have not come here on this dark rainy dawn to preach the dharma to puerile ignoramuses and ingrates!"

"AWAKE now, my precious brethren!"
"Come out of your samsaric sleep!"

Much to his surprise, everyone was indeed absurdly, insentiently, asleep.

"Up, up, up you get!"

"Let's get it on with a delicious bowl of 'prajna chompa', or wisdom gruel, sprinkled with Buddha bacon-bits, for this morning's breakfast of Chumps!"

"Brother Ananda, please do get the tea and fill-up the cups to Empty."

## Soda-Pop Buddha

"Bring to me your spirit and I will benevolently make it breathe with Life."

"Bring to me your heart and I will compassionately make it beat with Love."

"Bring to me your mind and I will clemently make it cogitate with Light."

"Well, will you just look at that... some soda-pop Buddha has got you by the left nostril, Watson!"

## The Passionate Experience of Boredom

"Do Zazen relentlessly now, and enervate yourself into thought free, conscious oblivion," snapped the Bodhidharma!

All expert sitting students who sit, sit, sit, desirelessly... eventually get to appreciate the passionate experience of boredom.

"Yep, sure was exciting, all right!"

Those were the last words of Master Jim-Po, who, in perfect posture of doing the practice of Zazen, passed away upon an insignificant, nonexistent atom, out of ordinary oblivion into pure Emptiness... boring even Death, to death.

The Neigh of Truth

## What's Cookin'

So what's cookin' in the Buddha's kitchen?
'Mindwaved Mu!', snaps the Cook.

## Chapter Eleven
### Plastered Wallflower, Meditating

The Boffola Belly of Bu'Tai

## The Mindful Fool

"The mindful Fool makes the forehead of Wisdom smile."

## Crazy Vitality

Vajrayana purity loves to fornicate with immorality, the end result being a true, crazy VITALITY.

*Eee-hah!*

The Boffola Belly of Bu'Tai

## The Open Palm

If you wisely give-up on the fact of the false self, and freely give away the (illusionary) ego, you gain the gift of the Open Palm.

Nothing is Real, really, yet everything is real.

And 'Being There' *Now*, you Bless and tranquilly rest, and Rest and blissfully bless.

## Quick Change

Quick change is always the rapid result of patient, hard dharma work.

*In less than no-time!*

The Boffola Belly of Bu'Tai

## The Expressed Letter

Clear visionary expression and pure radiant thought is but the expressed letter of the essentially inexpressible Buddha Mind.

Plastered Wallflower, Meditating

## The Spacious Invisible

The manifest pinpoint of visible life is but the condensed light of the Spacious Invisible, passionately desiring to be humanly punctuated.

*I'll be jiggered!*

The Boffola Belly of Bu'Tai

'Run'

Ubiquitous is the numinous Presence.
Run like hell.

## A Merry Mess

"Get out of my mindful meditation, Mary. Your mesmerizing moons are making my mind a merry mess."

*Holy Moly!*

The Boffola Belly of Bu'Tai

## Coldly Caught

A dull-yellow, plastered wallflower was coldly caught meditating upon a warm field of bright marigolds.

## Struck Blind

Get your face out of my blissfulness, your Highness,

You may just get struck blind by the blandness of my Niceness.

*Who would have thought!*

The Boffola Belly of Bu'Tai

## Kick Ass!

If you ask for it, pretty please...
Never fear, Master will kick ass!

Even if you don't (ask), he will anyway.

## The Lust In Us

Lord Jesus came to us because of the lust
He had for Life...

And lost His life because of the lust in us,
He came to Love.

The Boffola Belly of Bu'Tai

## Futuristic Man

Did Christ attain to Ecstacy sucking the Lovely Virgin breast.

Or did the Virgin get Blissed-out on the Christ, whilst suckling Him sweetly to her Bosom's divinely-nethered nipple... his minikin (baby) mouth bubbling forth a molten maelstrom of emancipative mantras... for futuristic man's mentally embodied hollow-head, to be worn on tall tuxedo shoulders?

Plastered Wallflower, Meditating

## Mary, Mary

If the Virgin Mary did it, why aren't you?
If the Virgin Mary didn't, why are you?

Day 71

## Young Buddha Abroad

If you say "No way, Jose!" to Buddha's gentle prod,

Then no way is the Way, my young buddha abroad.

However, do take this dual, yet consolidating counsel to mind:

"There seems to be no door to Liberation other than through the gateway of a cold, naked apperception of the No-self.

Only in the absolute absence of bare self-hood can compassion calmly contemplate Enlightenment."

*In phrasing an additional note to the above, it does seem true that only in the state of essential selfhood, where the No-Self is nakedly unveiled as an Absolute Absence, can there possibly be disclosed the No-Way of the Way, to an enlightened disciple's Awareness Void... of* PURE EMPTINESS.

## Dharma Defender

May kindness, beneficence, and benevolence bless my bare, un-sworded hand.

May Love take over the warrior bodhisattva body that I have just here-now, Become.

**Hail to Thee, O Noble Lord Manjushri:**

"May your breaking bread with the Sant Deva, Lord Michael,

Embrocate and sanctify my heart-mind with the full victory chant of:

>Jaya! Jaya!"

"And may the Divine Transmission of Warrior Wisdom going Beyond that which is Beyond...

Bring on the descending Blissful View of one-hundred-thousand crumbs of Awakened Compassion... which are to be gladly strewn,

By your newly knighted Dharma Defender, unconditionally free and radically wild...

Into the joyful Buddhafields of a yet sorrowful, and sorry samsara."

## Tie Me Up Mara!

Mind deliberates, karma clears the way, emptiness liberates, and the Buddha kicks ass.

Tie me up Mara, I want to be free!

## Flower of Wisdom

Wisdom cannot be won without the worn warriorship of a mortally wounded ego.

Knowledge is ever and ever, already passing.

Wisdom is always already, naturally immortal.

Illumined Bodhichitta is indeed, the saving seed and veritable crown of all Wisdom in man.

Real Wisdom's clarity and light shows up the Truth transparently in all worlds.

Desiring to learn, learning to learn, and knowing how to learn, are conditional to the humus, (and humor), of Wisdom's Light.

Despite its arcane age, Wisdom remains forever and ever young.

The Flower of Wisdom can only take root, and bloom in one place — the Injured Heart.

The Boffola Belly of Bu'Tai

## Zen Master, St. Claire

"Whether you defend yourself, or choose not to.

Whether you are guilty, or you are not.

Sixty slaps from my tongue.

Even so."

Day 66

Plastered Wallflower, Meditating

## Oh Fudge!

The formless forays forever for the form.

The form frantically fears the formless.

Oh fudge!

The Boffola Belly of Bu'Tai

## Unity and Diversity

Unity undresses into diversity, in order to divulge.

Diversity redresses into Unity, in order to rest.

Plastered Wallflower, Meditating

## One Verse

The Uni-verse is but one verse...
of the Buddha's speech.

Day 63

The Boffola Belly of Bu'Tai

## Sempiternally Stuck

Heaven and earth are eternally wedded.
Spirit and matter are sempiternally stuck.

Oh, s_ _t!

Plastered Wallflower, Meditating

Flowers

Ah, flowers from the garden are gently cut,

Kindly killed, to furnish a soft and chic decor.

Day 61

The Boffola Belly of Bu'Tai

## Man and Matter

Beat up on matter and you batter the Spirit.
Flagellate the man and you flail the Divine.

Day 60

Plastered Wallflower, Meditating

### World Tour

Movement permits Emptiness to scale the podium... that is, go out on a glitzy world tour.

*Hoist the blue Peter!*

# Chapter Twelve
## Baba Brain-Teasers II

The Boffola Belly of Bu'Tai

## The Peak of Silence

If you wish to understand Baba, let Baba Be your understanding.

For this, you must wait from the peak of Silence, or the mount of Naughtness, with all of your Being.

## An Absolute Absence

Baba can never be objectified. He Is the perfect Subjective You.

Baba Is an Absolute Absence positively existing as the Self of everyone, subjectively being Life.

*Aham Brahmasmi!*

The Boffola Belly of Bu'Tai

*Satchinanda!*

Unclasp the bridle of thought and you see not Baba... but Sat, Chit, and Ananda, as you.

*Mahanayarana!*

## Vision of Him

To have Baba's darshan is not to know Him, truly.

But to have vision of Him without seeing Him, is to Know Him, Truly.

*Sathyabela!*

The Boffola Belly of Bu'Tai

## So Near To His Heart

Why look for Baba when you are so Near to His Heart already Here.

## Brightly Anchored

Baba appears physically as an apparent Spiritual Being emerging out of your dependent need to be Saved.

But in essence, He is the very Absence of this world, already brightly anchored in your Heart, as Pure LOVE.

The Boffola Belly of Bu'Tai

## Baba Re-activates Baba

Every a.m. BABA re-activates Baba to create the comforting world of your seeing Him as LOVE serving your Self.

*Hanumanji Om!*

## The Pure Pleasure

Identify with your self, and you shall surely suffer.

Identify with Baba, and you shall surely suffer more...

But ah, the pure Pleasure.

The Boffola Belly of Bu'Tai

## Blank Barrenness

Brush (aside) Baba-the-body.

Bow to BABA the Buddha.

Believe in BABA the Blessed.

Bond with BABA the Bodhisattva.

Blend infallibly and absolutely with BABA, the Blank Barrenness.

## Sacrificial Becoming

Baba bore birth in order to make your beingness breathe with the bite of sacrificial Becoming.

*Tyaga, ah!*

The Boffola Belly of Bu'Tai

## Ochre Flame

Baba's blushing robe is an ochre flame of emblematic LOVE, circumambulating your Heart.

*Sita-Ram! Sita-Ram!*

## Babe of Abandon

Bond yourself to Baba as would a helpless babe of Abandon,

And reap you will, the wild wind of winged Wakefulness and wondrous Wisdom.

*Prajnasahaya!*

The Boffola Belly of Bu'Tai

## In Nakedness

"Give up your plush robes."
"In nakedness before Me come.
In absence before Me bow.
In Wakefulness before Me, die."

Day 46

## The Assurance

In Baba, the need to be loved dissolves into the assurance that you are Loved... body-mind, imperfections, and Nothing at All.

The Boffola Belly of Bu'Tai

## Just Aware Him

Baba is not a memory; therefore, do not continue to re-awaken Him within.

Baba is rather, the reality of your Truth being Love, and being Bared.

Hence, just Aware Him.

## The Golden Tremble

Baba's feet are deep-rooted in the tree of your Being.

As He Breathes, feel the Golden Tremble of the leaves.

The Boffola Belly of Bu'Tai

## Baba's Breath

The robotic mind intangibly obtrudes with Baba's Breath breathing Absence, No-Sense, and One-Taste into your body's noble temple.

## And Ah!

Take away the thought conceiving Baba and what is left is BABA, BABA, BABA ... and Ah!

The Boffola Belly of Bu'Tai

## No Hope

Once bound to Baba, do not try to bolt, there is no hope.

*Sai!*

## Your Lostness

Do not become in Baba; Be subtracted in Baba.

Pervade yourself not with His Presence; penetrate Him rather, with your Lostness.

## Truth

"I am a Teacher of Truth, I am a planter of Truth, I am a carrier of Truth.

I am the Light of Truth, I am the Sound of Truth; I am the road to Truth, I am the Transmitter of Truth.

I am the yearning for Truth, I am the suffering of Truth, I am the keening of Truth.

I am the Love of Truth, I am the Wisdom of Truth, I am the Reality of Truth — I Am The Truth, I AM THE TRUTH OF TRUTHS."

Can all this be true of Baba?

"TRUE as I AM VITTALA BLUE", replies BABA.

## Love Will Kill

If you do not interfere with the relationship of Baba and you,

Real Love will probably kill you, (as promised).

*Jaya! Jaya!*

## The Passion of Creation

Baba is not the existential film of a sensational Avatar, pressing upon the receiving plate of a personal consciousness, wanting to be saved.

He Is, rather, in Essence, the projectural Core of Consciousness Itself ...

Lightfully liberating the passion of Creation, (contractually-caught), within you.

## All Too Mortal, All Too Empty

Baba is the ultimate "kalyanamitra", (Spiritual Friend).

As I sweetly gaze upon His Glowing Face, His Glistening Grace, (kindly) exposes my self's many imperfections, and (cruelly) imposes my Soul's Divine Perfection... (upon this contrite, all too mortal, all too empty, human breast).

The Boffola Belly of Bu'Tai

### Behold B<small>ABA</small>'s Being

Abstract the past of the mind's memory of objects, and slash to ribbons the absences arising therefrom; and let the small self abstain from all self-expression, and let the spirit simply stand supremely Still... and in that eternal moment of suspended time in subtracted space... behold B<small>ABA</small>'s Being rushing in to fill-in the void, with Nothing but His bated B<small>REATH</small>.

## A Beloved Footprint

Do not glorify, (nor glamorize), BABA, and your relationship with Him.

Just keep diving deep into the Fullness of His Eyes... and (just keep) surrendering into a heap of nothingness at His Feet.

Keep subtracting your self, and selflessly become less and less, until the very empty spaces between His Toes, hollow-out into an irradiant Fullness within your mind.

And may His Eternal Essence compassionately overtake, (and drown), your being...

And leave a Beloved Footprint of Bodhisattvahood, upon your brilliant body.

CHAPTER THIRTEEN
QUINTESSENCE OF CREATION

The Boffola Belly of Bu'Tai

## Man Volunteered

It's easy, God first composed Himself...
and then man volunteered to be Created.

Day 32

## A Simple Penny

Once Division took place, multiplication just happened to happen to happen, and only the Single Mind can screech it to a halt, on a simple penny.

$$\div \times 1 \cent$$

### Just a Bit (Nearer)

Name the Name of the Adi Buddha's nature, and you cannot come near (Him).

Unname the Names of the Adi Buddha's empty attainments, and you come just a bit near(er).

## Permanency

Permanency permeates the impermanent impudently.

PHAT!

The Boffola Belly of Bu'Tai

## The Inaccessible

Why accede to the Inaccessible when the Inaccessible has access to us constantly.

Kye ho!

## Struck Blind!

Who has seen the Buddha has struck Him blind!

The Boffola Belly of Bu'Tai

## Vision of Buddha

Vision makes Buddha vanish and
the advent of Voidness inevitable.

Ah!

## Clamor of Chaos

Shunyata is the eternal crust of Quietness, covering the Quintessence of Creation... caught in the clamor of contractual chaos.

The Boffola Belly of Bu'Tai

Light

Light is the illumination of Ignorance, waved (aside) sometimes, as mere luminous immateriality — or the shining of empty Wisdom.

## Flatness Felt

Emptiness is the Flatness felt when the Creator-within has regurgitated the child of his manifest creation.

The Boffola Belly of Bu'Tai

## Yet To Be

That which is yet to be, is the Creator becoming that which He has not been — Already.

*Just imagine!*

## Creation

Creation can be uncreated, a BUDDHA cannot.

The Boffola Belly of Bu'Tai

And 'There J Was'...

The Unmoving moved into manifold manifest... and 'There I Was'... a renewed I am that just Became.

*(Wow!)*
*Fancy that!*

## Man Is Indubitably

The Radiant Lord is the Splendor of all that Is...
but man, is indubitably, the Master to become...
of all that Was.

The Boffola Belly of Bu'Tai

## No Holds Barred

The Buddha embraces all, no holds barred, with the All That He Is Not.

*I'll be!*

## Too Small, (or Too Big)

Divinity pours Itself *totally*,
into the smallest particle
of the Manifest.

Nothing is indeed too small, (or too big),
for it not to be stuffed to the full,
with the Divine.

Ah so, the Sufficiency of the Immensity.

The Boffola Belly of Bu'Tai

## To the Fullest

The Fullness of That Which Is Not fills everything to the fullest of that which Is.

*Will you figure that!*

## In Humble Cloth

The Light of the Verb may uphold the whole created universe; but on the other hand, the whole wide world is but the Little Buddha in humble cloth.

## Lone Source

The Radiant Lord's Light makes everything luminous.

The Absence of Light, however, makes for His Dark Shining...

And in time, unveils Him as the Lone Source of the REAL, 'That Is Naught'.

## Cede Control

Only after mastering yourself can the self dare surrender,

And confidently cede control to being Nothing short of Naught, Naturally Not.

The Boffola Belly of Bu'Tai

## Perfectly Impersonalized

The Summit of Silence impacts the peak of Spiritual Power, perfectly impersonalized.

## Unchangeable

The Master doesn't mind you keeping your Mind — it's unchangeable anyway.

*Check it out!*

The Boffola Belly of Bu'Tai

## Poor Me!

Pining for pleasure pins you piteously to pain.

Poor me! Poor me! Poor me!

*Poor orgasmic me!*

## Enough!

Enough with information, enough with knowledge!

From now on, your main mantra should be the efficient application of Wisdom gone Beyond, to the very edge of every moment of doingness, without doing.

The Boffola Belly of Bu'Tai

## Humus of Humility

Humbleness hones difficult, or great accomplishment, into the humanized humus of humility.

May the accumulated coproliths of all my actions, cosmically catch fire and be singed to essential ash, or sweet vibhuti.

Cow pies and heaps of humbleness are a cowman's, or commoner's, only hope for a fiery spirit and a warm heart.

## Do Not Become

Do not become a Master, just masterfully Be.

Do not become a Teacher, just simply Teach.

Do not become This or That, just clearly See.

## Advice To The Teacher
### (Which He May Ignore)

Too much bark and bite on the path, may bring on a morbidity of being.

Too much prohibition can conflagrate into a Jeanne d'Arc of smoky obsession.

Too much domination may gestate into a display of abject demotivation,

Too much authority may deteriorate into a sort of submissive absolutism.

Too much of anything really, is really too much of something,
Which may blow up into a radical case of too much airy aire,

Filling out the spaciousness of an essential Emptiness.

## The 'X' Factor

Because of the 'X' factor known as the All-Wise Unknown, the Future as an experimental Evolutionary Instructor, forces the sadhaka to work on deepening the wisdom of his personal relational skills... and not relate overly to that which is merely the manipulation of the correct facts, or the facile application of the science of (mere) knowledge, as applied to difficult, or sensitive situations.

Whenever it comes down to knowledge, truth, or Love, always... always pick Love, no matter what your educational bent, or your professional corridor of so-called correct cogitation.

At all times, choose Love, and not the power of being necessarily right, in the often refractive light of rational righteousness.

In short, Enlightened Bodhichitta, or Christ Love, is always synonymous with appropriate, correct and compassionate behavior, or rightly-inspired, charitable action.

The mysterious 'X' factor of the All-Wise Unknown abstracts hermetically, and without exception into the lilting, lavender, enigmatic Sphinx of LOVE... in relative relationship.

## Wherever Love Beckons

If you want to stay young, yet grow wise, be Attentive, be Attentive, and pay Attention.

Be aware, be loving, be kind, and most especially important, be not narcissistically, nor necessarily, always right.

Learn in all humility and with the awareness of an awakened Bodhichitta to be always compassionate and loving; and most importantly, to be honestly *really* wrong, instead of always, rightfully right.

Better to be wrong even when right, especially whenever and wherever, Love beckons.

Better to be dead wrong, if Love's light is livingly right, and presently pure.

Nor, should you ever forget the unerring wisdom of Discerning Love — for it is ever the Heart of No-Mind as Divine Essence, which guides you into the present moment of No-Time.

Be Attentive, be Attentive, and pay Attention!

## A Long Lavender Fart

If you can scratch your own bottom while looking at someone else's faults, you'll probably see your own manifold, polymorphic bloopers, clownishly and ceaselessly, somersaulting in a long Lavender Fart of Forever Samsara.

The Boffola Belly of Bu'Tai

## Skeleton in the Flesh

A skeleton sees another skeleton in the flesh.

Says he: "See you soon, Son."

## Rainbow Reality

The Mind is naturally mindless.

Consciousness is naturally un-conscious, (of being conscious).

And Spirit is spontaneously surprised, to be found in a zone of no-time at all.

So, be Natural.

Relax into the radiance of your Rainbow Reality — and there remain for the remainder of your natural Voidness, as it rains and rains nothing special and everything extraordinary, for the rest of your remaining years of impermanent living, just Aware-ing, and wearing your mendicant body of Light like an ordinary King of Creation.

Of naturally-wise Suchness is the nir-vana of samsara.

## Well, Blow Me Down!

Sky of Mind is the inherent open space of Awareness.

Well, blow me down, the wind there, is genuinely invisible.

Can 'Sky of Mind' make it free on its own worth, without the radical meltdown of the sense of self, or 'aham-kara'?

Indeed, for one and all it is Terminal Death.

How can anyone lose his way?

Well, blow me down again, the wind of Death was somehow, genuinely unexpected.

## So Natural

The essence of sky is infinity.
The essence of time is eternity.
The essence of space is emptiness.
The essence of emptiness is radiance.
The essence of essence is pure nothingness.

So natural.

All (in) Mind.
All Aware.
All Free.

How Can That Be?

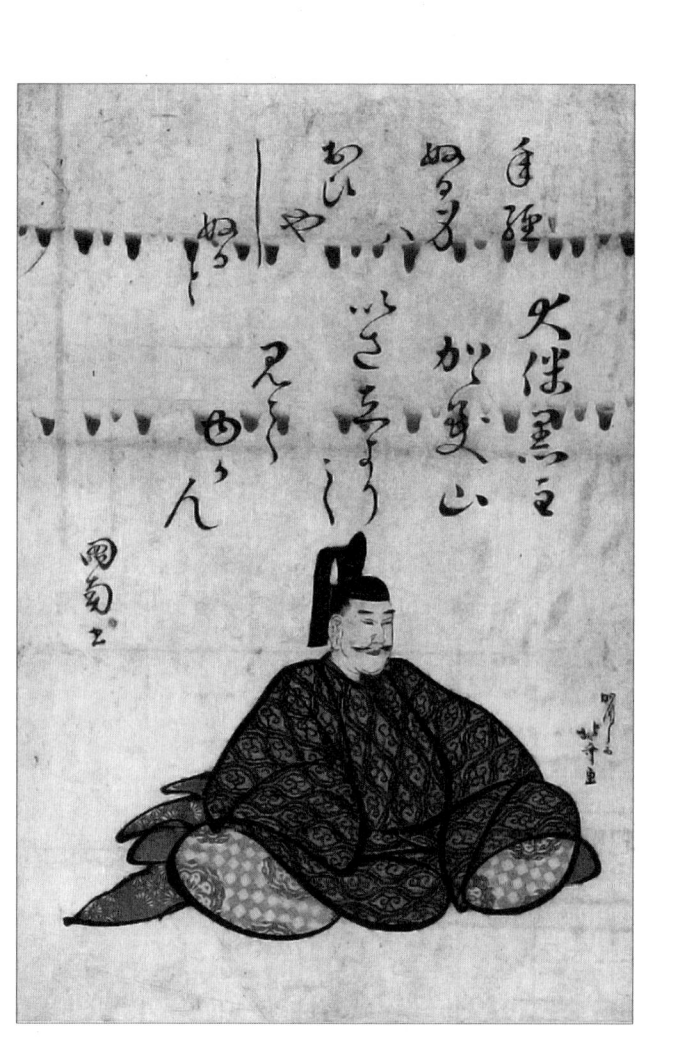

# Eructative Epilogue Epistle

# The Boffola Belly of Bu'Tai

## Natural Mind and No-Mind

Devoid of self-nature, all phenomenon that is apparent naturally relaxes, with nothing ever to prove, nor ever anything to maintain.

All apparent phenomenon, surprisingly and spontaneously, arises fresh as a newborn and shyly disappears with a contented baby sigh, evanescing imperceptibly into the Ineffable Suchness of Infinite Space.

Being factually elemental and everywhere evident, the phenomenon of phenomena is nowhere, nor ever, to be found incongruously contrived, in its purity of multi-variegated expression.

If somehow, there is by some divine slight-of-the-hand slip — oops — a mite intrinsic impurity somewhere present, (being, of course, almost always impossible to find), 'Things As They Are', as they abound naturally and creatively in manifest time, are just Effortlessly astounding, or perhaps, being a smite more correctly stated, are just supermundanely Simple.

But for all one knows, and maybe, in an effort to be more appercipiently accurate, the 'All That Is', can be purviewed as something sempiternally dynamic, always highly inspirational, and most commonly creative.

Agreed, there are times, when the 'All That Is' expresses Itself with lots of boom and brass, but then mysteriously, and every so often, It does so with just a bare whisper of a Breath, or with a serene, but brazen Absence of Presence.

And at rare other times, there simply shines everywhere a deep silence; and at even rarer times, there reigns ubiquitously a permutably profound peace — all so very Real, and yet, so Naturally Unreal.

As a rapturous incarnation of Mother MAYA, being divine, dramatic, and preternaturally creative, samsara could very well present in a first Mind scene, a most Solemn Void; in the second scene, a quiet Vibrant Vacuity; in the third scene, a crème de la crème of Divine Chocolate Essence; in the fourth scene, a hollow-headed, Hallowed Emptiness; in the fifth scene, a plain Blissful Nothingness; in the sixth scene, a complex Surrendered Simplicity; and in the final seventh scene, a pure Absolute Beauty that just makes you want to blush right out of existence.

# The Boffola Belly of Bu'Tai

Or, on a less blissful level, Mother MAYA, just for the sake of a playful leela, could mysteriously concoct a scene from out of the boisterous, obstreperous ghost of what was once old Louisiana, where unexpectedly, there sneaks quietly upon the ears… some lonesome whisperings of a somewhere-from-nowhere familiar sound of an otherworldly New Orleans band, phantasmagorically playing the 'Soham-Hamsa' Mantra in a surprisingly, divinely-rainbowed rhythm, or in a sad syncope of multi-colored, saintly-perfumed, sweet jazz.

Or metaphysically, as if by airy magic, SHE can create any surrealistic scene where there could even appear the irresistible phantasmagoric celebration of an All-Alabama musical scene with an irrepressible samsara rhythm, or a universal jazz-rag tune… starring, or light-spotting, the classical R. Charles singing the Blues, and sporting some totally uncanny black glasses for the Seeing Only.

Or, with a supernatural snap of HER fingers, the story could be all about the handing over of a magical, ornate, crystal conch shell as a metaphoric megaphone to some Blind Buddha… and hearing Him speak for openers, about how great it is, or would be, or always has been exhalting to See the Infinite Light of the Illimitable

Worlds without end... and there and then, invite us to make a brief pit pause in the famous, fictional red light district of the infamously incarnadine Immensity.

It is well known that the nondual state of Supreme (Radical) Awareness deposes a Secret Seal of incomparable, indelible Unity-Oneness upon the Buddhafields of both relative samsara and analogous nirvana.

The far too cryptic Zen koan of the slight of One-Hand-Clapping, can possibly (also) be accomplished with formidable dexterity and easy difficulty through the direct, (but far less well-known exercise), of the Yogini or Dakini arousal, (and release), of an unabashed, concentration of Bodhichitta energy, which unconditionally and compassionately embraces the Heart of Man. Of course, not to be forgotten within this scenario, is that the Hallowed Clap of Undivided Divinity cannot be heard without the eerie accompaniment and accomplishment of the Deva world, also generating forth an occult, unitive embrace of Mankind's Evolutionary Spirit.

The great Deva and Devi, (or Dakini) etheric kingdoms, working along with other divine dimensions of Light Beings and Spacious (Empty) Presences which cooperate in patrolling, protecting, and processing the Dzog-zen skies of Consciousness and Void, all joyously and with mindful awareness, take the risk of giving (Their) wholehearted recognition to subjective Man's creative, and passionate personality. Either foolishly-wise, or divinely confident, They simultaneously sanction the phantom reality of Man's physical Absence as being veritably valid, yet only, relatively true.

Yet, there is in Mankind, a non-rational, intuitive suspicion, and a potential (Impersonal) Realization, that the Descending View, or the Whole (Peep) Show, (if there Is one), is one that will always remain ever Pure, ever Free, ever Spontaneous, ever Abstract, and ever Real... in the total continuum and lost vastness of what seems to be... a dynamic, Empty Expanse in the Spatial SKY.

The whole phenomenal process of the continuity of Manifest Creation is, indeed, for Mankind, very sphingine and unusual, unparalled and unprecedented, unexplicably obscure and elliptically enigmatic.

The whole Magical Show of MAYA, being either created by GOD's Divine Touch, or at the behest of some Cryptic Energy's Powerful Will... somewhere at, or beyond, the outer limits of the Great Immensity's Ultimate Nature... can never be claimed as a personal thing, since It is even now and ever co-dependently arising, and It is spontaneoulsy happening, with or without you, or I, lifting a lone finger.

Supralogically, the 'All of It', cannot BE other than What It Is, as Essentially empty, Essentially expressionless, and Essentially inexpressible.

The All of It, Manifest and Unmanifest, will ever remain Beyond description, Beyond extinction, and Beyond even the highest of the Emptiness Wisdoms... without ever having been seen by the Natural Mind of anyone, nor even, by the great, Noble, No-Mind-At-All.

# Glossary

**Amitabha:** The Buddha of Boundless Bright.

**Aprajna:** Non-consciousness; prajna meaning 'wisdom', the sixth of the six perfections of the Bodhisattva path.

**Baba:** 'Father'; a term of affection for a saint or holy man.

**Bhajan:** Hindi devotional song expressing love for the divine; lit. 'adoration'.

**Bikkhu:** A fully ordained male Buddhist monastic; lit. 'beggar' or 'one who lives by alms'.

**Bodhgaya:** One of the four holy places of Buddhism; the place where Gautama Buddha attained Enlightenment under the bodhi tree. Called Uruvella in ancient times, and famous for being a place of Peace, Realisation and Enlightenment.

**Bodhichitta:** 'Awakened mind' or 'mind of enlightenment'; 'citta' signifies mind and heart, and 'bodhi' awake or enlightened; it entails the vow to attain enlightenment for the benefit of all beings; therefore, the Great Compassion.

**Bodhidharma:** He brought Zen Buddhism to China and is the first Chinese patriarch of Chan (Zen) lineage. He practiced unmovable zazen for nine years.

**Buddhafields:** Originates in the Mahayana Buddhist sutras; worlds of great beauty created by the compassionate action of a Buddha; an environment in which all the conditions are conducive to spiritual practice and enlightenment.

**Budh:** 'To awaken', 'to know', or 'to become aware'.

**Bu'Tai (Pu'Tai):** The Laughing Buddha known as Hotei (Japan) and Pu-Tai (China), and is regarded as an incarnation of Maitreya, the future Buddha. Pu'Tai was famed for his benevolent nature, (especially with children), as well as for his protruding stomach. He was said to travel everywhere with a hemp bag (a pu'tai) carried over his shoulder.

**Chela:** a term used in the Guru-shishya tradition of Hinduism, meaning disciple, student, or spiritual seeker.

**Darshan:** Being in the presence and receiving the blessing of a holy person, Master, or Guru.

**Dharmic (Dharma):** 'Divine duty', daily right action, the way of Truth, the cosmic law of Spirit; the 'great norm' underlying the manifested, or phenomenal world; finally, the inevitable law of underlying karmically-determined rebirth.

**Divya Atma Swaroopulaara:** One of the spiritual names of Sri Sathya Sai Baba, a highly revered spiritual leader, world teacher and Avatar; also a term used by Him tenderly in reference to His devotees.

**Dzogchen:** The primary teaching of the Nyingmapa school of Tibetan Buddhism. The natural, primordial state or natural condition of every sentient being; lit. 'great perfection', expressed in terms of Vision, Meditation and Action.

**Dzog-zen:** A new Dzogchen-Zen teaching whose goal is the direct experience, or sure sadhana, of spontaneously expressed Perfection; the spontaneous stance of natural Wisdom; the re-creation and stabilization of the incipient space of primordial Awareness.

**Emaho:** Exclamation of amazement, astonishment or wonder.

**Guru:** Spiritual Teacher/Preceptor/Instructor/Guide/Master; one who is mature, ripe, or 'heavy with the fruit' of Wisdom.

**Hanuman:** Hindu divinity representing the perfect disciple, who manifested in the form of a monkey; the devoted servant of Rama, his Lord.

**Ishwara:** Creator of the universe; the personification of the Absolute; Lord of the Manifest; the 'Lord' within man; a personalized, venerated form of the Lord.

**Kali:** A form of Shakti, as the embodiment of the Force of Destruction; Divine Wisdom which puts an end to all illusion. The Black One, the slayer of demons and the unreal.

**Karma (Karmic):** Destiny which is caused by past actions; law of cause and effect; action and reaction; 'as you sow, so shall you reap'.

**Kensho:** Zen expression for the inchoate, or incomplete experience of Awakening; lit. 'seeing suddenly one's own true nature'; one experiences the illusionary nature of the separate self.

**Koan:** A phrase from a sutra or teaching on Zen realization; lit. 'public notice'; a paradox, that which is 'beyond thinking', which transcends the logical or conceptual.

**Kokyu (-no-daiji):** Eureka! Another expression for the sudden but brief 'seeing-trough' of illusion; or a yet nascent, immature, howbeit intense, experience of Awakening; lit. 'great experience of one's own self'.

**Kundalini:** Occult energy stored primarily at the base of the spine. Its controlled, upward awakening (by the Consciousness) along the spine to the head's crown chakra, (Brahmarandhra), is one of the main goals of numerous spiritual traditions.

**Kwannon:** Avalokiteshvara, Mahakaruna Buddha, the Buddha of Great Compassion; also known in Japan as Kannon or Kanzeon, in China as Kuan Yin, and in Tibet as Chenrezi.

**Kye ho:** In its positive aspect it signifies an exclamation or invocation of astonishment, amazement, or wonder; therefore, meaning or referring to something 'wonderful'. In its negative sense, the phrase symbolizes an exclamation of distress, disconcertment, or disagreeableness; therefore, signifying something 'uncomfortable'.

**Kyeso:** Exclamation of distress, discomfort, and paradoxically also of appreciation; in another sense it may also mean something wonderful, amazing or marvelous; it can also be an invocation of astonishment, disconcertment or of wonder.

**Lama:** In Tibetan Buddhism, a religious master, or guru, an authentic embodiment of the Buddhist teachings; lit. 'none above'.

**Mahakala:** A fierce protector of Buddhism, a great guardian of the dharma (divine duty); symbolizes the death of negativities and the complete uprooting of negative patterns.

**Mahakashyapa:** One of the principal disciples of Sakyamuni Buddha; the first patriarch of the Ch'an/Zen tradition. He was renowned for his ascetic self-discipline and moral strictness.

**Maitreya:** The future World Teacher. He will inspire humanity to see itself as one family, and create a civilization based on sharing, economic and social justice, and global cooperation.

**Maitri:** Lit. 'kindness and compassion'; two principal Buddhist virtues that are the basis of the spiritual attitude of a bodhisattva (vow to bring all beings to liberation).

**Mara:** The Incarnation of the negative force in Buddhism; it also symbolizes the desires and passions which enslave man, as well as those obstacles, i.e., the (five) poisons, or passions, which impede his progress towards enlightenment.

**Mu:** Lit. 'nothing', 'naught', or 'have not'; used as a paradoxical response to certain koans and other queries in Zen Buddhism, intending to indicate that the koan or query itself is not the issue, but rather something else, or a quality, more abstruse.

**Murshid:** A God realized saint; a spiritual guide or Master.

**Nada:** 'Sound' or 'tone' and 'universal pulse of life' or 'flowing stream of consciousness'.

**Nirvana:** 'Nir' has a negative meaning of 'not' or 'no', and 'vana' means to 'flow'; therefore Nirvana denotes a primarily passive or negative state of 'non-flow'; traditionally, it connotes a taste of high enlightenment, where true liberation is released (departure from the cycle of rebirths) and integral oneness lived.

**Obaku:** Name of a fictitious Zen Master; one of the three Zen sects in Japan, founded in 1654 by the Chinese priest Yin-yьan Lung-ch'i.

**OM Mani Padme Hum:** 'OM, Jewel in the Lotus (of the Heart), Hum'; a well known mantra in Tibetan Buddhism; compassion mantra associated with Avalokiteshwara.

**Phat:** A Sanskrit term referring to the power to destroy and disperse.

**Poorna:** Complete, Highest, Whole.

**Prajnaparamita:** 'The perfection of wisdom', the wisdom of all Buddhas personified in the enlightened form of a female deity. The Prajnaparamita-Sutra is regarded as the holy mother that feeds the bodhisattva with the amrita (nectar) of prajna (transcendental wisdom).

**Prajnasahaya:** With wisdom as companion.

**Prarabdha karma:** Past karma which is responsible for the present body; 'actions begun, set in motion.'

**Prema:** Love of God; Love of Self; and Divine Love for all of creation.

**Roshi:** Title of a Zen Master; lit. 'old venerable master'; leads and inspires his students to eventual enlightenment.

**Sadhana:** Spiritual discipline and meditational practice; the duties and discipline of discipleship.

**Saecula saeculorum:** Latin, meaning 'for ever and ever'.

**Sahaja(m):** Innate, inborn; naturally or spontaneously Awake.

**Sai:** 'Master'; derivate of the Sanskrit word Swami.

**Samsara:** The wheel of rebirth, the process of worldly life; the cycle of rebirths that a being goes through within the various modes of existence until final liberation is attained.

**Sangha(s):** A Buddhist community or brotherhood; in common usage, a comradeship of similar souls upon a Spiritual Path.

**Sanyasin:** One who walks the path of Sanyasa ('renunciation', 'abandonment'), integrated into the spiritual world after renouncing all material life.

**Sathyabela:** Time of Truth.

**Sathyasya Sathyam:** Truth of Truths, which no one can visualise by the mind; it can only be experienced, not described.

**Satori:** Zen term for a more mature, or stable state of Awakening; individual Enlightenment.

**Sesshin:** Lit. 'collecting the heart-mind'; a retreat of intensive, strict practice of collected mind; meditation practice at a Zen monastery.

**Shunya:** Emptiness, Nothingness; Silence; the ultimate Reality as Void, or Voidness.

**Siddha:** A realized, Radical One; an accomplished yogin; one who has achieved superior mastery over the fiery elementals of the body and who has power over nature.

**Siddhartha:** The Buddha, born in the sixth century B.C. in what is now modern Nepal; the historical founder of Buddhism.

**Supasa:** Another name for Ganesha; 'with a good noose'.

**Tabla Rasa:** Latin for 'scraped tablet' or 'clean slate'; individual human beings are born with no innate mental content, ('blank'), and that their entire resource of knowledge is built up gradually from their experiences and sensory perceptions of the outside world.

**Tara:** A popular deity in Tibetan Buddhism, said to have issued from the tears of Avalokiteshvara in order to help him in his Task; she embodies the feminine aspect of Compassion.

**Tashi Delek:** Common, everyday Tibetan greeting honoring the self in other; Tashi means auspicious and Delek means fine or well; "auspicious greetings" or "may everything be well with you".

**Tathagata:** 'The thus gone one'; one of the ten titles of the Buddha, a term he used about himself as an individual who has brought an end to suffering and has reached nibbana (third noble truth).

**Teisho:** A Zen talk delivered by a Zen teacher often during intensive meditation retreats; lit. 'recitation offering, presentation'.

**Varagya:** Detachment, dispassion; non-attachment.

**Vica:** Stringed instrument.

**Yog:** Sanskrit word which means 'union'.

**Zafu:** Meditation cushion originally made out of cattail used by Zen Buddhist practitioners.

**Zazen:** Zen meditation; lit. 'seated mind'; the practice of awareness, of bringing your attention, or concentration, to the present moment.

Imprimé au Canada par
Transcontinental Métrolitho